Sustainability Reporting and Communications

Sustainability Reporting and Communications

Alan S. Gutterman

BEP
BUSINESS EXPERT PRESS
Leader in applied, concise business books

Sustainability Reporting and Communications

Copyright © Business Expert Press, LLC, 2021.

Cover design by Charlene Kronstedt

Interior design by Exeter Premedia Services Private Ltd., Chennai, India

First published in 2021 by
Business Expert Press, LLC
222 East 46th Street, New York, NY 10017
www.businessexpertpress.com

ISBN-13: 978-1-95253-896-4 (paperback)
ISBN-13: 978-1-95253-897-1 (e-book)

Business Expert Press Environmental and Social Sustainability
for Business Advantage Collection

Collection ISSN: 2327-333X (print)
Collection ISSN: 2327-3348 (electronic)

First edition: 2021

10 9 8 7 6 5 4 3 2 1

Printed in the United States of America.

Description

In order to know whether or not the corporate social responsibility (CSR) initiative and its related commitments are actually improving the company's performance, it is necessary to have in place procedures for reporting and verification, each of which are important tools for measuring change and communicating those changes to the company's stakeholders. Sustainability reporting should be broadly construed and has been described as communicating with stakeholders about a firm's economic, environmental, and social management and performance. Verification, often referred to as "assurance," is a related concept that involves measurement made through on-site inspections and reviews of management systems to determine levels of conformity to particular criteria set out in sustainability codes and standards to which the company may have agreed to adhere. While certain CSR and corporate sustainability disclosures have now become minimum legal requirements in some jurisdictions, in general such disclosures are still a voluntary matter and companies have some leeway as to the scope of their disclosures and how they are presented to investors and other stakeholders. This book is intended to be a practical introduction to sustainability reporting and communications that begins by discussing material legal and regulatory considerations and the some of the major sustainability reporting frameworks and then continues with detailed illustrations of how companies might create and distribute their sustainability reports and develop and implement their CSR communications strategies.

Keywords

sustainability; reporting; communications; CSR

Contents

CHAPTER 1

Introduction

In order to know whether or not the corporate social responsibility (CSR) initiative and its related commitments are actually improving the company's performance, it is necessary to have in place procedures for reporting and verification, each of which are important tools for measuring change and communicating those changes to the company's stakeholders. Hohnen and Potts described reporting as "communicating with stakeholders about a firm's economic, environmental and social management and performance" and verification, which is often referred to as "assurance," as a form of measurement that involves on-site inspections and review of management systems to determine levels of conformity to particular criteria set out in codes and standards to which the company may have agreed to adhere.[1] Verification procedures should be tailored to the company's organizational culture and the specific elements of the company's CSR strategy and commitments; however, it is common for companies to rely on internal audits, industry (i.e., peer), and stakeholder reviews and professional third-party audits. Verification procedures should be established before a specific CSR initiative is undertaken and should be included in the business case for the initiative.[2]

While certain CSR and corporate sustainability disclosures have now become minimum legal requirements in some jurisdictions, in general such disclosures are still voluntary and directors have some leeway with

---

[1] Hohnen, P., and J. Potts. ed. 2007. *Corporate Social Responsibility: An Implementation Guide for Business*. Winnipeg CAN: International Institute for Sustainable Development.

[2] Companies using the Future-Fit business goals recommended by the Future-Fit Business Network can adopt the "fitness criteria" associated with each of the goals. See the discussion of the Future-Fit business goals in *Future-Fit Business Framework, Part 1: Concepts, Principals and Goals* (Future-Fit Foundation, Release 1, May 2016), 25, FutureFitBusiness.org.

respect to the scope of the disclosure made by their companies and how they are presented to investors and other stakeholders. Some companies continue to limit their disclosures to those are specifically required by regulators; however, most companies have realized that they need to pay attention to the issues raised by institutional investors and other key stakeholders and make sure that they are covered in the disclosure program. At the other extreme, there are companies that have embraced sustainability as integral to their brands and have elected to demonstrate their commitment by preparing and disseminating additional disclosures that illustrate how they have woven sustainability into their long-term strategies and day-to-day operational activities. These companies understand that not only are investors paying more attention but that more and more people everywhere are considering environmental, social, and governance (ESG) performance when deciding whether to buy a company's products and/or work for a particular company and that it is therefore essential to lay out their specific CSR and corporate sustainability goals and the metrics used to track performance and provide regular reports to all of the company's stakeholders on how well they are doing against those goals.[3]

The scope of the company's reporting and verification efforts will depend on various factors including the size of the company, the stage of development and focus of its CSR commitments, legal requirements, the financial and human resources available for investment in those activities and the degree to which companies want and are able to integrate sustainability indicators into their traditional reporting of financial results. Ceres, a nonprofit organization advocating for sustainability leadership (www.ceres.org), has developed and disseminated its Ceres Roadmap as a resource to help companies reengineer themselves to confront and overcome environmental and social challenges and as a guide toward corporate sustainability leadership.[4]

---

[3] Expansive disclosure of this type increases the risk of litigation and/or adverse market reaction in the event that the company fails to meet its stated CSR and corporate sustainability goals, even if the disclosures are accompanied by appropriate disclaimers and are not included in regulatory filings that typically are covered by anti-fraud standards. Disclosure of actual or potential links between CSR and corporate sustainability goals and compensation must also be handled carefully, similar to links between short-term financial goals and compensation.

[4] Ceres. "The Ceres Roadmap for Sustainability" www.ceres.org/ceresroadmap

In the area of disclosure and reporting, Ceres stated that the overall vision was that companies would report regularly on their sustainability strategy and performance, and that disclosure would include credible, standardized, independently verified metrics encompassing all material stakeholder concerns, and details of goals and plans for future action. Specific expectations regarding disclosure were as follows:

- D1—Standards for Disclosure: Companies will disclose all relevant sustainability information using the Global Reporting Initiative (GRI) Guidelines as well as additional sector-relevant indicators.
- D2—Disclosure in Financial Filings: Companies will disclose material sustainability risks and opportunities as well as performance data, in financial filings.
- D3—Scope and Content: Companies will regularly disclose trended performance data and targets relating to global direct operations, subsidiaries, joint ventures, products, and supply chains. Companies will demonstrate integration of sustainability into business systems and decision making, and disclosure will be balanced, covering challenges as well as positive impacts.
- D4—Vehicles for Disclosure: Companies will release sustainability information through a range of disclosure vehicles including sustainability reports, annual reports, financial filings, corporate websites, investor communications, and social media.
- D5—Verification and Assurance: Companies will verify key sustainability performance data to ensure valid results and will have their disclosures reviewed by an independent, credible third party.

Cleveland et al. recommended that companies should align the manner in which sustainability issues are reported or communicated to stakeholders and others with the type and purpose of the report or communication. When reporting is mandatory, the applicable disclosure standards and guidelines promulgated by regulatory bodies such as the Securities and Exchange Commission (SEC) should be followed; however, when reporting is voluntary companies and their professional advisors must consider the standards and expectations of the audience, practices by other companies engaged in comparable business activities and the legal risks of disclosing "too much." Companies are generally admonished to disclose information that is "material" with respect to aspects of their business including environmental and social issues and risks, but Cleveland et al. pointed out that this is not necessarily a firm guide given the existence of differing concepts of materiality relevant to sustainability-related reporting that they summarized as follows[5]:

- Under the GRI reporting framework, information is considered material and should be included in a report if it "may reasonably be considered important for reflecting the organization's economic, environmental and social impacts, or influencing the decisions of stakeholders."
- The International Integrated Reporting Council (IIRC) deems information to be material if "it is of such relevance and importance that it could substantively influence the assessments of providers of financial capital with regard to the organization's ability to create value over-the short, medium and long term."
- For SEC reporting purposes and under the voluntary Sustainability Accounting Standards Board standards, information is deemed to be material if there is "a substantial likelihood" that a "reasonable investor" would view the information as "significantly alter[ing] the 'total mix' of information made available."[6]

Regardless of the particular standard applied to a specific sustainability-related report companies must ensure that disclosures are accurate and complete and this means creating an effective sustainability reporting and

---

[5] Cleveland, N., D. Lynn, and S. Pike. January 2015. "Sustainability Reporting: The Lawyer's Response." *Business Law Today*.

[6] Id. (citing *TSC Indus. v. Northway, Inc.*, 426 U.S. 438, 449 (1976)). Cleveland et al. explained that disclosures under the U.S. federal securities laws are a mixed question of law and fact and noted that it is the view of the SEC that the issuer is in the best position to know what is likely to be material to investors and that courts have opined that corporations are not required to disclose a fact merely because a reasonable investor would very much like to know that fact. Citing *Richman v. Goldman Sachs Group, Inc.*, et al., 10 Civ 3461 (June 21, 2012, United States District Court for the Southern District of New York). Id.

communication management system with disclosure controls and procedures, internal education and training, external review of proposed disclosures by legal counsel, and other professional advisors and continuous assessment to improve the reporting process.

In determining materiality and what should be covered in the sustainability report and how, consideration needs to be given to the input received from the company's external stakeholders. It has been observed that identifying poor quality and the costs associated with poor quality is a vital part of "triple bottom line" reporting and in order to do this companies must engage with each of their important stakeholders to understand the essence of the company's relationships with those stakeholders and what the stakeholders are looking for as indicators of value, integrity, and quality.[7] This means that companies need to take a hard and honest look at their impact on the communities in which they operate and quality of their relationships with employees, the products and services they offer to customers, their actions in the neighborhoods where their facilities are located, and footprint of their operations on the environment.

Jackson et al. counseled that companies should solicit comments and suggestions from individuals who were not involved in the original collection and assessment of the data used to compile the report and should ensure that all information that is proposed to be included in the report is rigorously checked for accuracy. Independent editing should be used to identify and remove details that are not vital to the report and any jargon that might confuse readers and the message that the report is supposed to convey. While the process of collecting data for a sustainability report is complex, the end product itself must be straightforward and understandable by all of the stakeholders, including stockholders, employees, community members, and business partners.[8]

---

[7] Jackson, A., K. Boswell, and D. Davis. November 2011. "Sustainability and Triple Bottom Line Reporting—What is it All About?" *International Journal of Business, Humanities and Technology* 1, no. 3, p. 58.

[8] Id. (citing Isaksson, R. 2005. "Economic Sustainability and the Cost of Poor Quality." *Corporate Social Responsibility and Environmental Management* 12, p. 197) (citing also Painter-Morland, M. 2008. "Triple Bottom-Line Reporting as Social Grammar: Integrating Corporate Social Responsibility and Corporate Codes of Conduct." *Business Ethics: A European Review* 15, no. 4, p. 352.)

When establishing plans for reporting and verification it is useful to obtain and review copies of reports that have been done and published by comparable companies. Reports of larger companies are generally available on their corporate websites and extensive archives of past CSR-focused reports can be accessed through various online platforms such as CorporateRegister.com, a widely recognized global online directory of corporate responsibility reports. It is also important to have a good working understanding of well-known reporting and verification initiatives such as the GRI Standards; the AccountAbility AA1000 series; the United Nations Global Compact; and the International Auditing and Assurance Standards Board ISAE 3000 standard. Country-specific information is also available through professional organizations such as the Canadian Chartered Professional Accountants, which has published an extensive report on sustainability reporting in Canada.

Reporting standards are also emerging for specific topics within the broader universe of CSR and stakeholder engagement. For example, while companies can use several of the disclosure categories in the GRI to describe their activities relating to community involvement, investment, and impact, they can also turn to a framework for reporting on corporate community investment promoted by the London Benchmarking Group (LBG) (http://www.lbg-online.net/), which is managed by Corporate Citizenship, a global corporate responsibility consultancy based in London with offices in Singapore and New York.[9] The LBG framework has been touted as an effective tool for quantifying and organizing information about corporate community investment and, most importantly, assessing and reporting on the impact of their relationships with communities and how to manage it. Other tools for reporting on community impact have included return on investment (ROI) frameworks; the social, ecological, and environmental footprints; the Ethos Indicators developed by the Ethos Institute and work done by partnerships between NGOs and multilaterals that have attempted to conceptualize impact related to broader sustainability dimensions.[10]

---

[9] 2014. *From Inputs to Impact: Measuring Corporate Community Contributions through the LBG Framework—A Guidance Manual.* London: Corporate Citizenship.
[10] 2008. *Reporting on Community Impacts: A survey conducted by the Global Reporting Initiative, the University of Hong Kong and CSR Asia.* Amsterdam: Stichting Global Reporting Initiative.

The scope and sophistication of CSR reporting has come a long way since the idea first came up in the mid-1990s, when only a handful of companies reported on social responsibility issues and activities in addition to their regular financial reports. Today almost all of the largest global companies produce reports on their environmental policies and activities, often providing interested parties with a whole range of documents that can be accessed in a separate yet highly visible section of the company website. Other international standards, such as the UN Global Compact, explicitly incorporate reporting as a fundamental requirement for demonstrating a commitment to sustainability. Specifically, companies participating in the Compact are required to make an annual "Communication on Progress" that outlines the actions they have taken with respect to integrating the Compact's ten principles and to make the communication publicly available to stakeholders through annual financial, sustainability, or other prominent public reports in print or on the company's website. The Compact recommends that companies follow the GRI Standards when preparing their reports.

Sustainability reporting is tightly connected with efforts to achieve global sustainability goals and targets such as the Sustainable Development Goals (SDGs) in the 2030 Agenda for Sustainable Development and the aspirations in other international agreements such as the Paris Agreement on climate change action because without reporting it is impossible to measure progress that has been made and what still needs to be done. In fact, the SDGs include a specific goal (Goal 12.6) to encourage companies to integrate sustainability information into their reporting cycles,[11] and research has been undertaken by the Global Reporting Initiative to identify concrete connections between sustainability reporting and SDG 1 (end poverty in all forms everywhere).[12] Other international standards, such as the UN Global Compact, explicitly incorporate reporting as a fundamental requirement for demonstrating a commitment to sustainability.

---

[11] The United Nations Environment Programme ("UNEP") and the Centre for Corporate Governance in Africa. 2016. "Carrots and Sticks: Global Trends in Sustainability Reporting Regulation and Policy (KPMG International, the Global Research Initiative ("GRI")." Available at: www.carrotsandsticks.net

[12] See Global Reporting Initiative. June 7, 2017. "Can Corporate Reporting Help End Poverty?" (encouraging companies to move beyond philanthropy and community engagement, toward strategies with large-scale impacts.)

Finnish Textile and Fashion (FTF), the central organization for textile, clothing, and fashion companies in Finland, noted that developing corporate responsibility is often seen as an internal quality assurance process, which the company wants to communicate to the outside world only when everything is taking good shape.[13] However, FTF pointed out that every step toward better performance is important and communicates where the company is heading and that for this reason companies needed to be prepared to begin communications with stakeholders regarding their corporate responsibility activities at the very earliest stages. This means that attention should be paid to reporting and communications when the first development plans are being prepared and the first targets and indicators are being established. Reporting and communicating on corporate responsibility at this point is a good way for companies to demonstrate their commitment to transparency, even though much of the work has yet to be completed or planned. Early reporting and communications should include information on deficiencies and problems that have been identified and the steps that the company proposes to take toward remediation including consultation with stakeholders impacted by a particular issue.

Purposes and Benefits of Sustainability Reporting

While many businesses engaged in sustainability initiatives because "it is the right thing to do," in most cases a sustainability-related action is significantly driven, at least initially, by some regulatory dictate. However, while regulators have been engaged in promulgating laws and regulations pertaining to the environmental aspects of the operational activities of companies for decades, they have been relatively slow to act with respect to mandatory sustainability reporting. As a result, sustainability reporting has emerged along a path of voluntary commitment, something that generally does not occur in the business world unless and until there is a solid positive link between the activity and economic growth. Moreover, sustainability

---

[13] 2016. *Finnish Textile and Fashion Corporate Responsibility Manual,* 55. Helsinki: Finnish Textile and Fashion.

reporting did not make sense unless companies had something material to report on, which met that sustainable activities needed to be integrated into business models. Absent a strategic commitment to sustainability, sustainability reporting risks being dismissed as a cynical marketing ploy ("greenwashing") rather than a sincere effort to sustain economic, environmental, and social growth.[14]

Assuming that companies had adopted sustainability-related related practices with respect to their operational activities and/or incorporated sustainability into their strategic decisions regarding products, services, and investments, they have come to realize that there are significant benefits and rewards from genuine sustainability reporting. A literature survey conducted by Mink found evidence to support the proposition that consumers recognize organizations that are truly sustainable and reward those organizations with their business.[15] Other reasons for sustainability reporting that have been cited by the world's largest companies include ethical and economic considerations, brand value, innovation and learning, employee motivation, organizational integrity and reputation, stakeholder inclusiveness and materiality, gaining competitive advantage, and cost savings through decreased resource consumption. Organizations seeking to fend off the negative effects of unethical behavior often turn to sustainability reporting as a means for demonstrating a remedial commitment to transparency.

One basic reason for sustainability reporting and verification is to make sure that the CSR initiative is properly managed and that persons involved understand they will be accountable for their actions. Other good reasons for reporting and verification include giving interested parties the information they need in order to make decisions about purchasing the company's products and/or investing in the company (the level of funding from investors focusing their interest on ethical businesses is continuously increasing) or otherwise supporting the company's community activities; collecting information that can be used to make changes and improvements to the company's CSR strategy and commitments; improving internal operations; managing

---

[14] International Survey of Corporate Responsibility Reporting. 2008. KPMG: Amsterdam, Netherlands.

[15] Mink, K. 2012. *The Effects of Organizational Structure on Sustainability Report Compliance.* Purdue University College of Technology Masters' Thesis. Available: http://docs.lib.purdue.edu/techmasters/62, 11.

and reducing risks; and strengthening relationships with stakeholders. Libit and Freier argued that CSR reporting provides companies with an opportunity to communicate their CSR efforts to the company's stakeholders, discuss certain successes and challenges with respect to the company on a wide array of CSR issues, demonstrate transparency, which can ultimately help to improve the company's reputation with certain stakeholders, provide existing and potential investors with CSR information to assist in analyzing investment decisions, and improve the effectiveness of ongoing shareholder relations campaigns such that activist shareholders are deterred from submitting CSR-related shareholder proposals or pursuing or threatening litigation.[16] However, in order to achieve the greatest benefits from reporting and verification, companies need to carry out those activities in a rigorous and professional manner using tools and standards that are widely recognized and accepted among those interested in the results.

A European Union publication encouraged companies to produce sustainability reports as a method for demonstrating transparency with regard to CSR that would ultimately build trust among customers, employees, and the local community, and help to strengthen the credibility of companies. The publication emphasized that this was important because trust binds existing customers and helps to win new ones in B2C (business to consumer) and B2B (business to business) transactions; trust increases the positive acceptance of the company by the local community and creates a good basis on which conflicts can be resolved constructively and successfully; and trust helps companies to attract the best brains and to keep employees. In addition, transparency has an internal effect and can help to identify business risks and optimize processes. The publication also noted that in the financial markets, a company's social and environmental performances play an increasing role in establishing stock value.[17]

According to Ernst and Young, sustainability reporting has emerged as a common practice of twenty-first-century business, moving well beyond a

---

[16] Libit, B., and T. Freier. 2013. *The Corporate Social Responsibility Report and Effective Stakeholder Engagement.* Chapman and Cutler LLP. Available at https://corpgov. law.harvard.edu/2013/12/28/the-corporate-social-responsibility-report-and-effective-stakeholder-engagement/

[17] European Union CSR for All Project. April 2014. *Handbook on Corporate Social Responsibility (CSR) for Employers' Organizations,* pp. 39–40.

few unusually green or community-oriented companies to acceptance among companies worldwide (e.g., almost all of the Global 250 issue sustainability reports) as a best practice. Organizations have learned that focusing on sustainability as part of their information collection and reporting processes helps them manage their social and environmental impacts and improve operating efficiency and natural resource stewardship. In addition, sustainability reporting is recognized as a vital component of shareholder, employee, and stakeholder relations and fosters investor confidence, trust, employee loyalty, and enhanced corporate reputation. Analysts often consider a company's sustainability disclosures in their assessment of management quality and efficiency, and reporting may provide firms better access to capital. Sustainability reporting is also an opportunity for companies to demonstrate that they are integrating a long-term perspective into their strategies and decision making, something that has become increasingly important to investors.[18]

Libit and Freier argued that CSR reporting provides companies with an opportunity to communicate their CSR efforts to the company's stakeholders, discuss certain successes and challenges with respect to the company on a wide array of CSR issues, demonstrate transparency, which can ultimately help to improve the company's reputation with certain stakeholders, provide existing and potential investors with CSR information to assist in analyzing investment decisions and improve the effectiveness of ongoing shareholder relations campaigns such that activist shareholders are deterred from submitting CSR-related shareholder proposals or pursuing or threatening litigation.[19] However, in order to achieve the greatest benefits from reporting and verification companies need to carry out those activities in a rigorous and professional manner using tools and standards that are widely recognized and accepted among those interested in the results.

Sustainability-related disclosures and reporting are also an important aspect of a company's overall drive to attain and maintain legitimacy and

---

[18] https://ey.com/us/en/services/specialty-services/climate-change-and-sustainability-services/value-of-sustainability-reporting

[19] Libit, B., and T. Freier. 2013. *The Corporate Social Responsibility Report and Effective Stakeholder Engagement*. Chapman and Cutler LLP, Available at https://corpgov.law.harvard.edu/2013/12/28/the-corporate-social-responsibility-report-and-effective-stakeholder-engagement/

preserve its social license to operation. A study of Chinese firms conducted by Dai et al. found that companies that had issued high-quality CSR reports were perceived as having greater legitimacy (operationalized by government endorsement and media endorsement) by the Chinese government and media, which in turn led to better financial performance.[20] Bachmann and Ingenhoff also found evidence to support the proposition that communicated CSR through disclosure activities had a positive effect on corporate legitimacy; however, they noted that the impact would likely be mitigated to some extent by stakeholder skepticism and distrust with regard to CSR disclosures.[21]

A 2013 article published in *The Guardian* reported on interviews conducted with a several of the world's sustainability reporting experts that were intended to collect their thoughts on the purpose of reporting in the then-current business environment.[22] One view was that the purpose of sustainability reporting was to answer the question of whether present practice can persist (i.e., continue to build more value than it destroys) and help companies find ways to become less unstainable. As such, it was essential that sustainability reporting actually measure progress toward achieving, and ultimately surpassing, sustainability by using real-world yardsticks such as the planetary boundaries. Another perspective was that sustainability reporting was the bedrock of serious CSR management systems and strategies and that reporting companies needed to be honest in their reporting and include negatives as well as positives in order for reporting to be carried out with integrity and become a driver of improved performance. Sustainability reporting was also recognized and praised as playing a vital role in reframing the meaning of value into something that is rooted in multiple capitals that encompass human, social, natural alongside financial. Another important

---

[20] Dai, N., F. Du, S. Young and G. Tang. Spring 2018. "Seeking Legitimacy through CSR Reporting: Evidence from China," *Journal of Management Accounting Research* 30, no. 1, p. 1.

[21] Bachmann, P., and D. Ingenhoff. September 2016. "Legitimacy through CSR Disclosures? The Advantage Outweighs the Disadvantages." *Public Relations Review* 42, no. 3, p. 386.

[22] Confino, J. May 23, 2013. "What's the Purpose of Sustainability Reporting?" *The Guardian* https://theguardian.com/sustainable-business/blog/what-is-purpose-of-sustainability-reporting

purpose of sustainability reporting cited by the experts was achieving a better understanding of the environmental and social problems confronting society in order to facilitate engagement with them and conversations among stakeholders on the best approaches to achieving sustainability.

Sustainability Reporting Research

Mink's survey of sustainability reporting research in 2012 led him to identify three main categories.[23] The first was country-level assessments, which focused on the quality of sustainability reporting within a particular country or among several countries, usually carried out by assessing the degree of sustainability report disclosure with respect to a particular reporting framework such as the GRI. A major international survey of corporate responsibility reporting conducted by and covering 22 countries found that every country reported to a varying degree of compliance and quality.[24] The second category was sector-level assessments, which had similar intentions to country-level assessment but were focused on a different unit of analysis. As was the case with the first category, fragmented reporting practices were the norm even when organizations claimed to be using the same reporting framework. The third category of research included efforts to assess particular reporting frameworks, generally with the goal of exposing shortcomings as a rationale for proposing a different framework. Mink also noted that researchers had touched on topics outside of the three main categories, such as determining the intrinsic and extrinsic motivations that influence organizations to voluntarily report sustainability efforts.[25] Mink's own research on

---

[23] Mink, K. 2012. *The Effects of Organizational Structure on Sustainability Report Compliance*. Purdue University College of Technology Masters' Thesis, 14–18. Available at http://docs.lib.purdue.edu/techmasters/62

[24] International Survey of Corporate Responsibility Reporting. 2008. KPMG: Amsterdam, Netherlands.

[25] Farneti, F., and J. Guthrie. 2007. "Sustainability Reporting by Australian Public Sector Organizations: Why They Report?" Proceedings of the Financial Reporting and Business Communication Research Unit 11th Annual Conference Financial Reporting and Business Communication Unit, Cardiff, Wales. (finding that providing information to internal stakeholders was the primary reason for developing sustainability reports and that the effort was spearheaded by one influential individual within the organization).

the characteristics that predispose organizations to produce more compliant sustainability reports also fell outside the three main categories and was driven in part by a desire to find a solution to the fragmentation in reporting practices uncovered in the other surveys in order to facilitate increases in sustainability report compliance that would contribute to brand value creation and produce meaningful results with respect to economic, environmental, and social sustainability.[26]

KPMG, the GRI, the United Nations Environment Programme (UNEP), and the Centre for Corporate Governance in Africa have partnered to compile and publish *Carrots and Sticks* as a comprehensive compendium of the global evolution of sustainability reporting/disclosure policy and regulation. The first report was published in 2006 and followed by second and third editions in 2010 and 2013, respectively. The latest edition of *Carrots & Sticks*, which was produced in 2016, was based on a review of the reporting landscapes in 71 countries and territories, including the top 60 economies by GDP and most Organisation for Economic Co-operation and Development (OECD) countries (note that the first edition in 2006 covered just 19 countries).[27] Of those countries, the researchers were ultimately able to identify some kind of sustainability reporting instrument (defined as any instrument, mandatory or voluntary, which requires or encourages organizations to report on their sustainability performance) in 64 countries, and the total number of instruments in force across all of those countries was almost 400. The report was structured to explore the following key questions:

- How many reporting instruments are in place?
- Are most reporting instruments mandatory or voluntary?
- Which organizations are issuing the most reporting instruments?
- Do these instruments cover all organizations or only specific types?

---

[26] Mink, K. 2012. *The Effects of Organizational Structure on Sustainability Report Compliance*. Purdue University College of Technology Masters' Thesis, 19–20. Available: http://docs.lib.purdue.edu/techmasters/62

[27] The United Nations Environment Programme ("UNEP") and the Centre for Corporate Governance in Africa. 2016. *Carrots and Sticks: Global Trends in Sustainability Reporting Regulation and Policy*. KPMG International, the Global Research Initiative ("GRI"). Available at www.carrotsandsticks.net.

- Do instruments require reporting in specific formats?
- How many reporting instruments focus on specific environmental or social factors?

The researchers acknowledged that sustainability reporting instruments can be categorized in several different ways. For example, instruments can be based on sustainability reporting requirements or expectations issued by governing bodies such as governments, financial regulators, or stock exchanges, and these regulations may be mandatory or voluntary and, in some cases, may be on a "comply or explain" basis. Self-regulation is also important and includes reporting requirements or expectations issued by organizations (e.g. industry organizations) to apply to their own communities or memberships. In addition, consideration must be given to requirements, guidance, or recommendations for public reporting on single topics, such as greenhouse gas emissions, or a specific sector, such as mining. Finally, companies often choose to base their sustainability reporting on voluntary guidelines and standards and implement one of the major sustainability assurance standards to lend credibility to their reporting efforts. The reporting itself occurs in a number of different ways including in annual financial or sustainability reports, on websites, in documents submitted to a stock exchange for listing purposes and in data published in response to questionnaires and specific regulations.[28]

Some of the key findings in the 2016 report included the following[29]:

- There had been a surge in the number of reporting instruments identified since the last report in 2013, with growth being particularly strong in Europe (which continued to have a clear lead among the regions in terms of the overall number of instruments in place, not surprising given that sustainability reporting and associated instruments are more mature in Europe than in other regions), Asia Pacific, and Latin America.[30]

---

[28] Id. at 8.
[29] Id. at 9.
[30] Id. at 11.

- Government regulation accounted for the largest proportion of sustainability reporting instruments worldwide with governments in over 80 percent of the countries studied in the research introducing some form of regulatory sustainability reporting instrument through laws such as company acts and accounting regulations, often after a period in which the regulated topics had been addressed through voluntary efforts of companies in those countries.
- Mandatory instruments dominated (two thirds of the identified instruments were mandatory) but growth in voluntary instruments was also strong.
- Around one in ten instruments, both mandatory and voluntary, adopted a "comply or explain" approach, and the researchers noted that this approach, even when applied to voluntary instruments, can result in a higher level of sustainability reporting due to the effects of peer pressure.
- Governments issue the most sustainability reporting instruments, but not all of those instruments mandate sustainability reporting (e.g., national action plans relating to corporate social responsibility, sustainable development, business and human rights); however, activity among stock exchanges and financial market regulators was growing and together they were responsible for almost one third of all sustainability reporting instruments, including codes of conduct and standards, identified.
- Almost one third of reporting instruments applied exclusively to large listed companies and of these around three quarters had been introduced by financial market regulators and stock exchanges; however, around 40 percent of the instruments applied either to all companies (without distinction by size, listing, or sector) or to all companies except state-owned enterprises.[31]
- More countries are exploring expansion of reporting instruments to small- and medium-sized enterprises, some of which are voluntarily expanding their reporting in response to peer pressure from the actions of larger companies; however, policymakers need to

---

[31] Id. at 16.

consider the impact of mandated reporting on smaller enterprises that will struggle to comply due to resource constraints.[32]

- While most of the reporting instruments covered all sectors (i.e., cross-sectoral scope), those that targeted specific sectors addressed the finance and heavy industry sectors in particular.
- Governments and regulators increasingly required or encouraged companies to disclose sustainability information in their annual reports, a trend this is consistent with pressures from financial institutions, notably institutional investors, for improved information about the material relevance of sustainability risks.[33]
- There was a large increase in instruments driving reporting of social information (e.g., human rights, supply chains, conflicts materials, labor and employment, etc.), and the number of instruments identified by the researchers that focused on reporting of social information had almost doubled since 2013, growing faster than instruments that focused on the reporting of environmental information.
- Regulation on tax disclosure increased as companies came under increasing pressure to demonstrate that they were paying their fair share of taxes in all countries in which they operate.

In their conclusions to the report the researchers acknowledged the significant progress that had been made over the 10 years since the project began with respect to the geographic, sectorial, and topical scope of sustainability reporting; however, they cautioned that it was essential for the bodies that issue reporting instruments to focus on coordination and harmonization, which would require increased levels of collaboration and joint commitments between these bodies. Companies should also expect to contend with complex and difficult issues of prioritization and materiality with respect to the sustainability reporting activities, particularly since the expectations of stakeholders relating to transparency are expanding to include a broader range of sustainability issues such as taxation and human rights.[34]

---

[32] Id.

[33] Id. at 18.

[34] Id. at 22.

Organizational Structure and Sustainability Reporting

Mink conducted qualitative research to determine the organizational characteristics that contribute to developing sustainability reports that were compliant with the most rigorous requirements of the GRI.[35] Results from a survey of 107 organizations that had received an *A* + GRI application level in 2010[36] suggested that there is a relationship between an organization's genuine commitment to sustainability by their leadership and a sustainability report's compliance level. Mink also reported that the research implied a relationship between the sustainability expectations of stakeholders and the sustainability report compliance level and that the combination of leadership commitment and stakeholder expectations promoting a sustainability-minded culture within the organization that facilitated the production of sustainability reports. In other words, leadership determination to satisfy stakeholder expectations drove the creation of organizational culture and processes that served as the foundation for high-quality sustainability reporting. The compliant companies were also noteworthy for their ability to overcome resource constraints to complete the reporting process and to recognize the value of the market incentives generated by the development of a sustainability report. Mink noted that it did not appear that the participating organizations necessarily strived for a particular GRI compliance level, but that their sustainability

---

[35] Mink, K. 2012. *The Effects of Organizational Structure on Sustainability Report Compliance.* Purdue University College of Technology Masters' Thesis. Available: thttp://docs.lib.purdue.edu/techmasters/62

[36] The third generation of the GRI guidelines ("G3") was in effect in 2010 and provided for incremental guideline application in recognition of the varying levels of sustainability maturation among organizations seeking to implement the GRI framework. Mink explained: "The G3 Guidelines differentiate between levels of application by assigning corresponding letters ranging from A to C. Level A application represents the highest level of compliance to G3 Guidelines, followed by level B and level C. By completing external assurance, organizations can further increase the level of application, which is represented by appending a plus sign (+). For example, if an organization was fully compliant with the G3 Guidelines and solicited external assurance, the organization would receive an application level of an A+." Id. at 13. The three levels of compliance were removed in subsequent generations of the GRI framework.

report compliance level ultimately emerged from the development of a genuine sustainability culture and the associated sustainability commitment.[37]

Management Philosophy

One of the most interesting and useful conclusions reached by Mink based on his research was that the leadership of an organization (i.e., the managers, general manager, vice president, president/CEO, and the board of directors), as evidenced by demonstration of a genuine awareness and commitment for sustainability reporting, dictated the success of such reporting within that organization.[38] The *A* + compliant organizations participating in the survey vested primary responsibility for sustainability reporting at the manager or greater hierarchical position and charged that person and position with initiating sustainability reporting, being the strongest advocate for continuing sustainability reporting and providing final approval for the publication of sustainability reports. In so doing, according to Mink, the foundation was laid for creating and strengthening a sustainability culture, thus providing unique opportunities to institute sustainability reporting expectations, establish significant weight for reporting initiatives, and encourage greater reporting compliance.

The majority of the respondents to the survey (71 percent) pointed to more than one individual for assuming this responsibility and included responses such as: "Sustainability Manager, Communications manager, representatives from key business units"; "Corporate Environmental Affairs Manager, Sustainability Reporting Manager, and Group Environment Manager"; "CSO and CR reporting mananger [*sic*]." Among the groups of individuals that were provided as being responsible for designing and implementing the sustainability report, there were common themes of specific titles mentioned, the most prominent of which included Sustainability Manager, Communication Manager, Chief Sustainability Officer, Sustainability Reporting Manager/Social Reporting Director, CFO, and Investor Relations Manager. Mink noted that the main impression to be taken from the responses was that respondents overwhelmingly decided to place responsibility for sustainability

---

[37] Id. at 57.
[38] Id. at 49.

reporting in the hands of someone who held the title of a manager or above in the organization's hierarchy.[39]

Stakeholder Engagement and Improved Operational Sustainability

Management philosophy and its related influence on the company's organizational culture were driven by an important motivator: the desire to incorporate the expectations of stakeholders regarding sustainability activities and reporting thereon. Mink found that 62 percent of participating organizations declared that stakeholder engagement and inclusiveness was the top motivator for voluntary development of a sustainability report. As such, representatives of the organization, starting with the leadership, invested time and effort in consulting with stakeholders to identify sustainability report content and develop reports that were not only compliant with the GRI framework but also useful to stakeholder consumers of the information. Stakeholder inclusiveness has long been one of the fundamental principles of the GRI framework. Survey participants identified other motivators for sustainability reporting, the second most important of which was the value that reporting offered as a management tool to improve sustainability within their organization. Specifically, the respondents indicated that their sustainability reports aided in improving data quality, diagnosing the status of sustainability within the organization, and ensuring improvement on stakeholder sustainability concerns.[40]

Stakeholder engagement also played an important role in ensuring that a response was given on each core indicator in the then-current GRI reporting framework with due regard to GRI's materiality principle. In fact, stakeholder engagement/involvement was the most common approach in determining materiality within the surveyed organizations. The second most common method used by the respondents was external assurance, which was not surprising given that all of the respondents were A + GRI applicants and thus were required to rely on external assurance in order

---

[39] Id. at 42.
[40] Id. at 37–38 and 49.

to be eligible for receiving an *A* + application level. Other methods used by the responding organizations included checklist comparisons (e.g., GRI sector supplement checklists, internal checklists, and indicator questionnaire checklists), discussions with key subject experts, alignment of organizational strategy with the GRI indicators, benchmarking the trend of best practices, materiality reviews, discussions among members of an internal sustainability board, and surveying company managers about key sustainability issues.[41]

Resource Availability

The organizations participating in the survey reporting a wide range of human and financial resources committed to the development of their sustainability reporting processes; however, most of the organizations did not appear to have "adequate" resource availability, meaning that overcoming resource availability constraints was generally a real challenge to achieving the highest level of sustainability reporting compliance.[42] However, organizations were still able to produce an *A* + sustainability report by relying on reporting motivations, organizational culture, and several other strategies to succeed. For example, organizations reported that they were able to build sustainability reporting into their other reporting requirements through report integration that focused on reducing information overlap and ensuring that data was readily available for usage in all of the company's reports: financial, regulatory, and sustainability. This allowed companies to save valuable time, reduce the amount of resources required for effective overall reporting and focus their efforts on preparing reports that were highly compliant. Mink noted that experience in preparing sustainability reports was also a factor in the quality of the reports, as 77 percent of participating organizations had completed five or more GRI sustainability reports. Mink noted that the GRI's creation of three levels of compliance was intended, at least in part, to allow organizations to adopt the reporting framework gradually and most toward higher levels of compliance (C to B to A) gradually as they mastered the basics.

---

[41] Id. at 44–45.
[42] Id. at 50–51.

Market Incentives

Competence in sustainability reporting was encouraged and supported by organizational realization and acceptance of various market incentives for improving the level of reporting compliance. Participants in Mink's survey mentioned that their level of effort with respect to sustainability reporting was motivated by improving stakeholder engagement, increasing transparency, strengthening company values and integrity, and increasing brand value, all of which were market incentives that benefited not only the organizations financially and operationally but also society as a whole.[43]

Challenges for Sustainability Reporting

The respondents to the survey of 107 organizations described earlier also indicated that the biggest challenge they faced in their sustainability reporting practices was data capture and information flow, a problem that became even more difficult to overcome when organizations grew in size and their scope of their operations became global.[44] The second most commonly mentioned challenge was resource constraints, including financial, human, and time. Other issues for the respondents included "defining materiality" due to a lack of set standards and regulations for establishing materiality, constantly changing information and topics of importance, and establishing the specific concerns of stakeholders; the lack of support and consensus ("especially from the CEO") within the organization; risk-aversion (i.e., publishing areas of poor performance), employee and customer engagement, integrating financial data and sustainability performance, and integrating the sustainability report into daily operations.[45]

A 2013 article published in *The Guardian* reported on interviews conducted with a several of the world's sustainability reporting experts that were intended to collect their thoughts on various topics relating to sustainability reporting including shortcomings of then-current sustainability reporting

---

[43] Id. at 51.

[44] Id. at 35–36.

[45] Id. at 36.

practices and the steps that might be taken to address them.[46] One of the experts was particularly interested in the emergence of integrated reporting as a transition from the previous practice of preparing and distributing separate sustainability reports while retaining the traditional annual report focused almost exclusively on financial matters. He argued that companies should use integrated reporting as an opportunity to addressing stakeholders beyond those targeted by the integrated report (i.e., financial capital providers); provide details on the company's competitive positioning in the emerging sustainability space; provide more detailed coverage of the company's initiatives relating to social, human, and natural capital; and develop online reporting methods that were more comprehensive and closer to delivering real-time ESG data. Another expert viewed sustainability reporting as a means for companies to gather further knowledge about nonfinancial risks and opportunities and encouraged companies to disclose those in their reporting along with discussions that demonstrate the steps that are being taken to manage them. One intriguing viewpoint was that integrated reporting at the company level, while valuable, was not sufficient to building resilient and equitable economies and that efforts needed to be made to integrate reporting across supply chains, stock exchanges, and economies, with meaningful links to societal and biosphere health. Finally, several of the experts stressed the purpose of sustainability reporting as being conversation: stirring engagement and debate among people and institutions about what needs to be done to address sustainability challenges. In other words, reporting is not simply about what has happened in the past—a dry compendium of metrics on carefully selected environmental and social performance indicators—but also a catalyst for deliberation on further actions and a foundation for planning and executing those actions.

Another challenge for the future of sustainability reporting also comes with significant opportunities for companies that are adequately prepared to invest the time and resources required to harness the explosion of data relating to sustainability-related topics. It has been suggested that digital data on sustainability will be the main tool for companies make strategic

---

[46] Confino, J. May 23, 2013. "What's the Purpose of Sustainability Reporting?" *The Guardian*, https://theguardian.com/sustainable-business/blog/what-is-purpose-of-sustainability-reporting

decisions regarding their sustainability policies and procedures and companies will be able to take advantage of almost real-time data created by businesses and governments that is shared across open platforms. As a result, sustainability disclosures are expected to change significantly in the years to come including a formal shift from annual reporting to the frequent exchange of sustainability data, a move toward the macro challenges faced by society, placement of the supply chain into the spotlight, and a new role for stakeholders who will be empowered by the information to engage in real-time interactions through various channels.[47]

While some obligations to report nonfinancial information are sometimes imposed by law and regulation, and thus not something that a company can avoid, in most companies embark on sustainability reporting as a voluntary undertaking after engaging in serious internal debate about whether such reporting is feasible and the impacts it is likely to have on the company's operations and profile in the eyes of stakeholders. Companies need to understand that once sustainability reporting has started, it cannot be deferred or halted with loss of image. In other words, preparation of a sustainability report is not a one-off event, but the beginning of an ongoing obligation that must be permanently integrated into the way in which the company operates and communicates internally and externally.[48] In addition, sustainability reporting must be done in alignment with proactive environmental and social initiatives by the company so that the company has a good "story to tell" to stakeholders regarding improvements in its environmental footprint and contributions to social causes. If the company's social commitment is declining and/or its economic impacts are getting worse, sustainability reporting, if done properly with balanced attention to both the good and bad, will bring significant problems into the public light. Finally, while there is still no universally accepted framework for sustainability reporting, best practices are emerging and it is clear that companies are expected to invest sufficient resources in reporting to product reports that are meaningful to stakeholders and satisfy principles of quality such as those

---

[47] Hespenheide, E. September 2016. *A New Era of Corporate Disclosure*. Ernst and Young.

[48] *Handbook on Corporate Social Responsibility (CSR) for Employers' Organizations* (European Union CSR for All Project, April 2014), 44.

included in the GRI framework: accuracy, balance, clarity, comparability, reliability, and timeliness.

Role of Audit and Disclosure and Reporting Committees

Every company that becomes subject to the periodic disclosure requirements of the, as amended (such companies are generally referred to as a "reporting company" and/or "public company") will be expected to prepare annual reports; quarterly reports; current reports and annual reports to shareholders. Companies that have become subject to the disclosure rules must also comply with the Exchange Act's disclosure requirements relating to a wide range of other corporate governance activities including solicitation of proxies, tender offers, and "going private" transactions. In addition, directors, officers, and principal shareholders of reporting companies are subject to disclosure requirements relating to their ownership interests and changes in those interests. The disclosure requirements associated with public company status can become quite burdensome to the company; however, the ability to access the public capital markets carries with it the responsibility to adhere to the guidelines of the SEC and the stock exchanges with respect to disclosure and protection of shareholder rights.[49]

The SEC has granted public company audit committees substantial authority and responsibility with respect to compliance with the disclosure

---

[49] Filing a registration statement under the Securities Act of 1933, as amended, subjects most such registrants to the periodic reporting requirements of the Exchange Act, which are subsequently discussed, due to the application of Section 15(d) of the Exchange Act. However, those registrants that are not also registered under the Exchange Act are not subject to disclosure requirements governing various corporate governance activities including solicitation of proxies, tender offers, and going private transactions and, in addition, officers, directors, and principal shareholders are not subject to reporting of their ownership interests or changes in those interests. These disclosure requirements would, however, become applicable when the company is required to register its securities under the Exchange Act (or does so voluntarily). If a company equals or exceeds certain minimum requirements with respect to total assets and/or number of shareholders as of the end of any fiscal year, or its security is to be traded on a national securities exchange, then registration under the Exchange Act will be required.

and reporting process. Accordingly, the audit committee should always be a central player in the preparation and review of reports and other disclosure documents, as well as the certifications that must be given by the senior managers (i.e., the CEO and CFO). In most instances, boards do not create separate disclosure and reporting committees and provide for all disclosure and reporting matters to be overseen by the audit committee alone. In those situations, the audit committee itself may create a subcommittee that focuses on disclosure controls and preparation of required and voluntary reports. For the sake of separating out disclosure and reporting from all the other issues that an audit committee must handle, the following discussion pertains to any board-level body specializing in disclosure and reporting (referred to generally as the "disclosure and reporting committee"), be it a subcommittee of the audit committee or a standalone board committee.[50]

As part of their efforts to demonstrate compliance with corporate governance principles to their investors, disclosure and reporting committees should adopt and publish various policies and procedures relating to their disclosure processes and internal controls. For example, a policy statement on disclosure processes and procedures may describe the disclosure process used by the company, including the creation of an internal disclosure committee and appointment of a disclosure controls monitor, and a detailed description taken to ensure that disclosure documents are complete and accurate. A statement of policies and procedures regarding internal controls and risk management may be used to describe the principal activities of the company's internal controls or audit function including risk assessment, development of control strategies, implementation of monitoring procedures, and communication of information to senior management, the disclosure and reporting committee, and the entire board of directors.

---

[50] For discussion of the duties and responsibilities of the audit and disclosure and reporting committees, see "Audit Committee" and "Disclosure and Reporting Committee" in "Governance: A Library of Resources for Sustainable Entrepreneurs" prepared and distributed by the Sustainable Entrepreneurship Project (www.seproject. org).

Role of Lawyers in Reporting

While sustainability reporting has its roots in voluntary disclosure as opposed to fulfilling specific legal and regulatory requirements, all types of reporting raise potential legal risks that will require counseling from attorneys familiar with traditional disclosure concepts such as "materiality" and "reasonable investor" and with the emerging marketplace for sustainability-related nonfinancial information and the frameworks for disclosure of such information that have been rapidly evolving. Park noted that attorneys can help companies assess the materiality of nonfinancial information relating to sustainability and evaluate the risks of disclosing, or not disclosing, such information, and provided a list of some of the issues relating to disclosure of nonfinancial sustainability-related information that attorneys may be asked to opine upon by their clients[51]:

- What kind of nonfinancial information should be provided, in what level of detail, and in what format?
- Should the company provide information only on ESG issues that investors have specifically asked about or should the company provide information on the commonly sought types of information (e.g., climate change) for companies in its industry?
- How much nonfinancial information and at what level of detail (e.g., general initiatives or measurable performance) is enough to satisfy investors?
- Should the nonfinancial information be provided in voluntary sustainability reports or in SEC filings?
- What should be the role of the board of directors in overseeing collection, analysis, and reporting of nonfinancial information, given that such information is related to risk mitigation and value creation?

---

[51] D. Park, "Investor Interest in Nonfinancial Information: What Lawyers Need to Know," *Business Law Today* January 2015.

- What procedures should be put in place for reporting on nonfinancial information by management to the board and should the board form a separate committee to oversee disclosures and disclosure controls and procedures related to nonfinancial information?
- What changes should be made to existing disclosure controls and procedures, as well as management and employee training, to account for the need to collect and analyze data necessary for effective disclosure of nonfinancial information?
- Should the compensation of executives be tied to performance on nonfinancial matters and, if so, for how long a time period and using what metrics?

CSR Reporting for New and Small Businesses

Smaller businesses generally do not have the resources to engage a professional auditor or prepare elaborate reports on their CSR activities; however, this does not mean that small businesses should avoid attempting to implement some basic and relatively simple steps for reporting the results of their sustainability efforts. The GRI has argued that transparent reporting and communicating about sustainability initiatives and programs creates valuable internal and external benefits for new and small businesses.[52] Among the internal benefits that were noted were the following:

- *Forging and Describing Vision and Strategy:* By placing their purpose, vision, and strategy into the context of global sustainability during the course of the sustainability reporting, new and small businesses can establish a direction for their activities and make that direction clear and explicit for their stakeholders.
- *Developing Effective Management Systems:* In order for sustainability management and reporting to be effective, new and small businesses must invest in the development of management systems that can track and analyze data and use the results to

---

[52] *Small Business Big Impact: SME Sustainability Reporting from Vision to Action* (Amsterdam and Geneva: Stichting Global Reporting Initiative and the International Organization of Employers, 2016), 3. The publication is available for download at www.globalreporting.org.

identify and exploit opportunities for improvement, efficiency, and cost savings.

- **Identifying Strengths and Weaknesses:** Committing to reporting and communicating drives managers of new and small businesses to seek out early warning signs of emerging issues that provide a chance to grasp opportunities and address potentially damaging developments before they grow into problems that threaten the survival of the organization.

- **Recruiting and Motivating Employees:** Communication, including reporting, is essential for recruiting and motivating employees through engagement in sustainability, leading to a workforce that is loyal and committed to the organization and its mission.

Important external benefits to new and small businesses from sustainability reporting and communication include building goodwill and reducing reputational risk; improving product image and branding; signaling quality and good management that leads to new sources of capital and reduced costs of financing; building or restoring trust among stakeholders through increased and improved stakeholder engagement; and increased customer satisfaction and loyalty, leading to more opportunities to collaborate with business partners as members of their trusted supply chain network.

Hohnen and Potts suggested that small companies could take several modest steps to report and verify their CSR initiatives[53]:

- While it is probably impractical to appoint a full-time CSR executive, small companies should at least designate one senior employee to monitor CSR activities and collect information that can be used to develop new CSR initiatives and report activities to stakeholders (the designated employee's existing duties and performance metrics should be rearranged to accommodate the CSR-related activities).

---

[53] P. Hohnen (Author) and J. Potts (Editor), *Corporate Social Responsibility: An Implementation Guide for Business* (Winnipeg CAN: International Institute for Sustainable Development, 2007), 72.

- A modest budget should be set up to cover anticipated CSR activities and key people in other departments (e.g., human resources, customer service, marketing and public relations, manufacturing, etc.) should be asked to submit ideas for CSR projects and informed that they will be expected to work with the designated CSR employee on projects from time-to-time.
- Even if the company has not yet adopted one of the international CSR instruments, information regarding its CSR activities should be posted on the company's website and should include both successes and areas that have been targeted for improvement.
- Information on CSR activities can also be communicated to customers, suppliers, and other business partners and community members by adding new sections to the company's brochures and pamphlets and posting pictures of activities that can be viewed by visitors to the company's facilities.
- Information about the company's CSR activities can be placed in local newspapers, a relatively easy and low-cost public relations effort that has high impact among current and prospective employees, local customers, and community members.
- Staff briefings on CSR activities should be held on a regular basis and small businesses should also invite business partners and community members to events at the company's facilities, which showcase some of the things that the company is doing with respect to CSR.
- CSR should be placed on the agenda for all discussions with key customers, suppliers, and other business partners in order to gather their input and ideas on things that the company can do in the CSR area and get feedback on current initiatives.
- Small businesses should begin with a self-assessment of CSR commitments using well-accepted global guidelines as a reference point and use the self-assessment process as a means for preparing for more rigorous verification and reporting in the future.

CHAPTER 2

Legal and Regulatory Considerations

Sustainability reporting refers to the preparation and dissemination of disclosures pertaining to "nonfinancial information," which has been described by Park as including information relating to climate change, water quality and quantity, ethical business practices, cybersecurity, and supply chain management as well as narrative discussions of what the company considers to be the material environmental, social, and governance risks to its business and how the company is managing those risks.[1] Park described the background for the views of the Securities and Exchange Commission (SEC) on whether nonfinancial information was material to a reasonable investor and thus required to be disclosed because it would be important to the investor's investment decisions. Park noted that during the late 1960s and early 1970s shareholders and other organizations were beginning to ask companies to disclose more information on social, environmental, and civil rights performance as well as product safety and design issues. In 1971, the National Resources Defense Council asked the SEC to expand civil rights and environmental disclosure under the federal securities law in a rule-making petition; however, after almost a decade of investigations and public hearings, the SEC declined to make the requested changes based on its conclusion that they were not needed because only a small fraction of investors considered social and environmental information to be important. The SEC was also reluctant to move away from its long-standing economic understanding of materiality and to require disclosures solely for the goal of changing corporate behavior.[2]

Park went on to point out that the level of investor interest in non-financial information had dramatically increased since the SEC's market

---

[1] Park, D. January 2015. "Investor Interest in Nonfinancial Information: What Lawyers Need to Know." *Business Law Today*.

[2] Id.

study of the 1970s. Among the reasons that Park cited for this transformation were the growth of sustainable, responsible, and impact investing; changing attitudes of investors, analysts, and portfolio managers, a large majority of which had come to believe that nonfinancial information was pivotal in their investment decision making; significant dissatisfaction among investors with the quantity and quality of disclosures of social and environmental information[3]; and the greater presence of long-term oriented institutional investors as owners of the largest public companies in the United States and the growing commitment of those investors to incorporating sustainable, responsible, and impact principles into their investment analysis and decisions regarding allocation of capital.[4]

Cleveland et al. noted that when companies get started with sustainability reporting, they have a number of basic questions: "What are we legally required to communicate?" "What are we permitted to communicate?" "What can or should we say to stay competitive and protect business relationships, profitability and our social license to operation?" "What standards

---

[3] According to a 2014 survey conducted by PricewaterhouseCoopers (PwC) and cited by Park, the areas of greatest dissatisfaction among investors with respect to disclosures by U.S. companies included comparability of sustainability reporting between companies in the same industry; relevance and implications of sustainability risks; sustainability strategy that is linked to business strategy; internal governance of sustainability issues; the process used to identify material sustainability issues. Id. (citing PwC, Sustainability Goes Mainstream: Insights into Investor Views (May 2014).

[4] According to Eccles and Rogers, investors were incorporating environmental, social, and governance information into their fundamental equity analysis in several ways: economic analysis: to understand industry trends and externalities likely to affect the economic outlook and, therefore, value creation and capital formation; industry analysis: to understand factors driving competitiveness and the potential for sustained value creation in an industry as well as externalities from an industry likely to affect other industries (and therefore portfolio risks); company strategy: to understand management quality and corporate strategy, and evaluate a company's ability to respond to emerging trends; and valuation: to adjust traditional valuation parameters and assumptions, including cash flow and weighted average cost of capital, to reflect performance on material sustainability issues. R. Eccles and J. Rogers, *The SEC and Capital Markets in the 21st Century: Evolving Accounting Infrastructure for Today's World* (Washington, DC: Governance Studies at Brookings, September 2014), 5 (as cited in D. Park, "Investor Interest in Nonfinancial Information: What Lawyers Need to Know", Business Law Today (January 2015)).

should we use?"[5] They pointed out that many companies start down the path of sustainability reporting primarily as a marketing strategy, hoping to address the questions from customers and demonstrate social responsibility and philanthropy as part of an effort to build reputation. However, as the information is made available, companies must be prepared to defend it by responding to demands for verification and "ratings" released by organizations that often do not seek input from the companies that they evaluate. At the same time, investors are likely to have questions regarding the matters covered in sustainability reports and companies can expect that they will soon be asked to expand their reporting beyond their own activities to include their supply chains. Very quickly what may have begun as a project in the marketing department expands into a multidisciplinary initiative that will require support from across the organization and development of a comprehensive communications program with all of the company's stakeholders to ensure that the sustainability reporting is adequately addressing all of their reasonable needs and expectations.

Williams noted that to the extent that governments have regulated corporate responsibility per se, such regulation has focused on disclosure and during the period 2000 to 2015 over 20 countries enacted legislation to require public companies to issue reports including environmental and/or social information.[6] Many of these countries are in Europe and the European Union has implemented a directive that requires approximately 6,000 large companies and "public interest organizations," such as banks and insurance companies, to "prepare a nonfinancial statement

---

[5] Cleveland, N., D. Lynn and S. Pike. January 2015. "Sustainability Reporting: The Lawyer's Response." *Business Law Today.*

[6] Williams, C. 2016. "Corporate Social Responsibility and Corporate Governance." In *Oxford Handbook of Corporate Law and Governance*, eds. Gordon, J, and Ringe, G, 15. Oxford: Oxford University Press. Available at http://digitalcommons.osgoode. yorku.ca/scholarly_works/1784 (citing Initiative for Responsible Investment, Corporate Social Responsibility Disclosure Efforts by National Governments and Stock Exchanges (March 12, 2015), Available at http://hausercenter.org/iri/wpcontent/ uploads/2011/08/CR-3-12-15.pdf). These countries included Argentina, China, Denmark, the EU, Ecuador, Finland, France, Germany Greece, Hungary, India, Indonesia, and Ireland (specific to state-supported financial institutions after the 2008 financial crisis), Italy, Japan, Malaysia, The Netherlands, Norway, South Africa, Spain, Sweden, Taiwan, and the UK.

containing information relating to at least environmental matters, social and employee-related matters, respect for human rights, anti-corruption and bribery matters."[7] In addition, several stock exchanges around the world require social and/or environmental disclosure as part of their listing requirements including exchanges in Australia, Brazil, India, South Africa, and the London Stock Exchange.[8] Also, pension funds in countries such as Australia, Belgium, Canada, France, Germany, Italy, Japan, Sweden, and the UK are required to disclose the extent to which the fund incorporates social and environmental information into their investment decisions.[9] All things considered, surveys show that more and more jurisdictions are implementing mandatory environmental, social, and governance (ESG) disclosure requirements and that "there is a clear trend towards an increasing number of environmental and social disclosure requirements around the world."[10]

The United States, which has comprehensive reporting requirements relating to a broad range of corporate governance matters, has been a notable laggard with respect to establishing a comprehensive general ESG disclosure framework. However, while ESG- and CSR-related reporting is not yet specifically required for companies with shares listed on the U.S. exchanges, by 2013 more than half of the companies in the S&P 500 had

---

[7] See 6 of Directive 2014/95/EU of the European Parliament and of the Council of 22 October 2014, amending Directive 2013/34/EU as regards disclosure of non-financial and diversity information by certain large undertakings and groups, Official Journal of the European Union L330/1-330/9.

[8] Williams, C. 2016. "Corporate Social Responsibility and Corporate Governance." In *Oxford Handbook of Corporate Law and Governance*, eds. Gordon, J. and Ringe, G., 16. Oxford: Oxford University Press, available at http://digitalcommons.osgoode.yorku.ca/scholarly_works/1784 (citing Initiative for Responsible Investment, Corporate Social Responsibility Disclosure Efforts by National Governments and Stock Exchanges (March 12, 2015), available at http://hausercenter.org/iri/wpcontent/uploads/2011/08/CR-3-12-15.pdf).

[9] Id.

[10] Id. at 19 (citing KPMG, UNEP, Global Reporting Initiative and Unit for Corporate Governance in Africa, Carrots and Sticks: sustainability reporting policies worldwide 8 (2013), available at https://globalreporting.org/resourcelibrary/carrots-and-sticks.pdf

voluntarily decided to report and disclose ESG and CSR information[11] and so-called sustainability reporting is well on its way to becoming an expected standard practice that must be added to oversight agenda of the entire board and the disclosure and reporting committee. The committee will need to not only understand emerging voluntary reporting standards, such as those developed by the Global Reporting Initiative (GRI), but must also monitor developments in other jurisdictions, such as the EU and countries in Asia, where regulators have been much quicker to implement formal require-ments relating to ESG and CSR reporting that may ultimately become the foundation for expanded regulations in the United States.[12] For example,

---

[11] Libit and Freier reported a dramatic increase in CSR-related reporting among S&P 500 companies from 2010, when approximately 20 percent of the companies pro-vided such reporting, to 2012 when 53 percent of the companies reported on their CSR activities. B. Libit and T. Freier, *The Corporate Social Responsibility Report and Effective Stakeholder Engagement* (Chapman and Cutler LLP, 2013), Available at htt-ps://corpgovlaw.harvard.edu/2013/12/28/the-corporate-social-responsibility-report-and-effective-stakeholder-engagement/ (citing 2012 Corporate ESG/Sustainability/Responsibility Reporting: Does It Matter? Analysis of S & P 500 Companies' ESG Reporting Trends and Capital Markets Response, and Possible Association with De-sired Rankings & Ratings, Governance & Accountability Institute, Inc. (2012)). The KPMG Survey of Corporate Responsibility Reporting 2013 surveyed an even bigger group consisting of over 4,100 companies and found that 71 percent of them were reporting on CSR. KMPG also reported that among the world's largest 250 compa-nies, the reporting rate was 93 percent. Interestingly, however, only 5 percent of the companies were reporting on how environmental and social risks could impact their financial results and only 10 percent reported on linkages between CSR and executive compensation. As cited in H. Gregory, "Corporate Social Responsibility," practicallaw. com (April 2014).

[12] As a practical matter, it may not matter whether U.S. regulators actually mandate a specific CSR-related disclosure because if non-U.S. companies are providing such disclosures due to regulations in their home jurisdictions global institutional investors, who are comparing opportunities across borders, will effectively demand comparable disclosures by U.S. companies seeking their capital. A powerful and useful resource for monitoring actions regarding sustainability reporting among stock exchanges around the world is the United Nations' Sustainable Stock Exchanges (SSE) initiative (http://www.sseinitiative.org/), which is a peer-to-peer learning platform for exploring how exchanges, in collaboration with investors, regulators, and companies, can enhance corporate transparency—and ultimately performance—on ESG (environmental, social, and corporate governance) issues and encourage sustainable investment. Among

the listing rules for the Singapore Exchange require every listed company to prepare an annual sustainability report on its sustainability practices, with reference to five primary components (i.e., material ESG factors; policies, practices, and performance; targets; sustainability reporting framework; and board statement) on a "comply or explain" basis.[13]

In 2017, nearly 7,000 companies in the European Union became subject to expanded requirements for covering ESG matters in their annual financing reports including new disclosures on human rights impacts, diversity, anticorruption policies, and environmental matters. When preparing their reports, companies are expected to describe their business model and the outcomes and risks of their policies. Larger companies are also required to include and evaluate information on their supply chains, which means that smaller companies that act as suppliers to the reporting companies will need to expand their own data collection and information reporting activities even though they are not directly subject to the public reporting requirements. Canadian securities regulators have explicitly expanded the general requirement that public companies must disclose all material information to include material information regarding environmental and social issues and issued guidance on what information regarding environmental matters needs to be disclosed.

In the United States, the federal Securities and Exchange Commission (SEC) has struggled in its attempts to prescribe requirements for reporting on sustainability matters in filings that must be made by public companies. For example, with respect to climate change, the SEC

---

other things, the SSE has compiled a summary table of the sustainability reporting measures in place within G20 Members and by board members of the International Organization of Securities Commissions. Areas evaluated include the source of sustainability reporting initiatives, the scope of the reporting application, the scope of the subject matter, and the disclosure model.

[13] "SGX Sustainability Reporting Guide" in Sustainability Guide for Boards: At a Glance (Singapore Institute of Directors, KPMG and SGX, September 2017). The listing rules provide that the board is collectively responsible for the long-term success of the issuer and in exercising such responsibility the board has duties to provide strategic direction and specifically consider sustainability issues as part of its strategic formulation and to determine the environmental, social, and governance factors that are material to the business and see to it that they are monitored, managed and reported upon.

promulgated Release No. 33–9106, *Commission Guidance Regarding Disclosure Related to Climate Change* (February 2, 2010), which suggested that climate change disclosures might be provided in response to certain disclosure items in Regulation S-K such as Description of Business (Item 101 of Regulation S-K), Legal Proceedings (Item 103 of Regulation S-K), Risk Factors (Item 503(c) of Regulation S-K), and Management's Discussion and Analysis of Financial Condition and Results of Operations (Item 303 of Regulation S-K). The Release called on companies to consider disclosures on the following matters relating to climate change: the impact of legislation and regulation regarding climate change, including the potential impact of pending legislation; when material, the impact on their business of treaties or international accords relating to climate change; whether legal, technological, political, and scientific developments regarding climate change will create new opportunities or risks, including reputational risks; and the actual and potential material impacts of the physical effects of climate change on their business, such as the effects of severe weather, sea levels, arability of farmland, and water availability and quality.[14]

Other sustainability-related areas in which the Congress, the SEC, and state lawmakers have required disclosures include the sourcing of certain "conflict minerals"; payments to governments by resource extraction issuers; business with certain governments, persons, and entities subject to specific U.S. trade sanctions; releases into the environment; management through recycling; median employee pay; and mine safety disclosure.[15] Directors need to be involved in decisions regarding placement of CSR and corporate sustainability disclosures including links in SEC filings to online sustainability reports and adding sustainability information to proxy statements as part of the company's

---

[14] Cleveland, N., D. Lynn and S. Pike. January 2015. "Sustainability Reporting: The Lawyer's Response." *Business Law Today*.

[15] Id. See also Williams. C. 2016. "Corporate Social Responsibility and Corporate Governance." In *Oxford Handbook of Corporate Law and Governance*, eds. Gordon, J and Ringe, G, 16–19. Oxford: Oxford University Press, Available at http://digitalcommons.osgoode.yorku.ca/scholarly_works/1784; and Williams, C. 1999. "The Securities and Exchange Commission and Corporate Social Transparency." *Harvard Law Review* 112, 1197.

investor-focused communication efforts. Companies can, and often do, rely on communications professionals to prepare sustainability reports; however, even when such reports are not included in the company's SEC filings, they should be subject to the same level of scrutiny applied in procedures established by the board's disclosure committee.

Cleveland et al. reported on several ratings systems and screen tools that investors regularly consult to assess how companies manage their environmental and social impacts including the Bloomberg ESG Valuation Tool and its ESG Score; MSCI's ESG Impact Monitor; the FTSE-4Good Index; GS SUSTAIN and CDP reporting framework, all of which rely heavily on the nonfinancial information that companies provide in their mandatory and voluntary reporting.[16] Companies can expect to see an increase in legally mandated sustainability reporting as stakeholders continue to pressure lawmakers and regulators to improve the quality and consistency of reporting on sustainability-related issues beyond what companies have been providing on a voluntary basis. It will become easier for governmental decision makers to accede to these pressures as consensus emerges on appropriate reporting standards, since these can be integrated into any new legal requirements.[17]

Proposals from shareholder activists often help create the list of CSR and corporate sustainability topics that garner the most attention from companies and trigger movement toward greater transparency and disclosure. In recent years, companies have frequently been required to respond to call for changes in corporate policies and activities with respect to political and lobbying activity, sustainability reporting, gender pay gap reporting, and child labor issues.[18]

---

[16] Cleveland, N., D. Lynn and S. Pike. January 2015. "Sustainability Reporting: The Lawyer's Response." *Business Law Today*.

[17] For background on the debate in the United States regarding the appropriate amount and format of sustainability-related disclosures in SEC filings, see the letter from the Business Law Section of the American Bar Association to the SEC dated December 15, 2017 regarding Business and Financial Disclosure Required by Regulation S-K Release No. 33–10064; 34–77599; File No. S7-06-16) (generally endorsing the SEC's traditional "principles-based approach" to reporting requirements for its flexibility but acknowledging that there may be circumstances where the SEC should prescribe ESG disclosures that integrate both principle-based and prescriptive disclosure elements).

[18] Gregory, H. July 1, 2017. "Corporate Social Responsibility, Corporate Sustainability and the Role of the Board." *Practical Law Company*, p. 4.

In many cases, companies have been able to calm the concerns of activists, sometimes getting them to withdraw their proposals, by promising to provide fuller disclosure; however, once a commitment is made to expanded disclosure, the company needs to fulfill its promises and allocate sufficient resources to the effort since activists will be watching closely to ensure that their expectations are satisfied. When formulating voluntary CSR-related disclosures, it is important to engage with activists to ensure that they understand the approach that the company is willing to take and the company's need to balance disclosure against the need to protect sensitive and strategically important information.

A large number of parties providing comments to the SEC on its April 2016 concept release on disclosure required by Regulation S-K, the prescribed regulation under the that provides the framework for mandated disclosures in filings with the SEC, recommended that CSR disclosure be expanded and strengthened.[19] While it is not likely that more CSR-related disclosures will be formally mandated in the immediate future, companies must nonetheless give greater consideration to CSR and corporate sustainability when responding to several current items in Regulation S-K include those related to describing the business activities of the company (Item 101); legal proceedings (Item 103); disclosures of material known events and uncertainties in the Management's Discussion and Analysis (Item 303) and risk factors (Item 503(c)). Public companies must also be mindful of the SEC's guidance regarding disclosures relating to climate change, which was issued in 2010[20], and Rule 13 p-1 under the relating to conflicts materials disclosure.

In addition, companies may be subject to disclosure requirements under the laws of foreign countries in which they operate as well as various state and local laws. For example, under the[21], which went into effect on January 1, 2012, every retail seller and manufacturer doing business in California and having annual worldwide gross receipts that exceed $100 million is required to disclose its efforts to eradicate slavery and human trafficking from its direct supply chain for tangible goods offered

---

[19] Sustainability Accounting Standards Board. 2016. "Business and Financial Disclosure Required by Regulation S-K—the SEC's Concept Release and Its Implications." 3–4, available at sasb.org.

[20] SEC Release Nos. 33–9106, 34–61469, FR-82 (February 8, 2010).

[21] California Civil Code § 1714.43.

for sale. The disclosures must be posted on the retail seller's or manufacturer's website with a conspicuous and easily understood link to the required information placed on the business' homepage. In the event the retail seller or manufacturer does not have a website, consumers must be provided the written disclosure within 30 days of receiving a written request for the disclosure from a consumer. At a minimum, the disclosures should disclose to what extent, if any, that the retail seller or manufacturer does each of the following:

- Engages in verification of product supply chains to evaluate and address risks of human trafficking and slavery. The disclosure must specify if the verification was not conducted by a third party.
- Conducts audits of suppliers to evaluate supplier compliance with company standards for trafficking and slavery in supply chains. The disclosure must specify if the verification was not an independent, unannounced audit.
- Requires direct suppliers to certify that materials incorporated into the product comply with the laws regarding slavery and human trafficking of the country or countries in which they are doing business.
- Maintains internal accountability standards and procedures for employees or contractors failing to meet company standards regarding slavery and trafficking.
- Provides company employees and management, who have direct responsibility for supply chain management, training on human trafficking and slavery, particularly with respect to mitigating risks within the supply chains of products.

The exclusive remedy for a violation of the disclosure obligations is an action brought by the California Attorney General for injunctive relief.

CHAPTER 3

Sustainability Reporting Frameworks

In order to assure the quality of sustainability reporting and facilitate the efficient creation of comparable reports, it is necessary to have robust reporting standards that can be applied in a global economy in which the operational activities and reporting responsibilities of companies transcend national borders. International organizations, such as the United Nations (UN); regional organizations, such as the European Union (EU); and stock exchanges and independent organizations, such as the Global Reporting Initiative (GRI), have all been involved in the development and implementation of key international initiatives on sustainability reporting. Many of these initiatives take the form of national policies and instruments that incorporate elements of international or corporate social responsibility reporting frameworks. For example, The GRI Standards are referenced in government or market instruments in dozens of countries around the world, such as the preamble of the EU Directive on disclosure of nonfinancial and diversity information, and are frequently one of several normative or management standards referred to in reporting instruments, usually accompanied by references to the UN Global Compact, Organisation for Economic Co-operation and Development (OECD) Guidelines for Multinational Enterprises and the ISO 26000 Guidance Standard on Social Responsibility.[1]

There are a variety of frameworks and tools that organizations can leverage in order to develop their sustainability strategies and reporting processes. Many of these take a comprehensive approach and have

---

[1] Carrots and Sticks: Global Trends in Sustainability Reporting Regulation and Policy (KPMG International, the Global Research Initiative (GRI), the United Nations Environment Programme (UNEP) and the Centre for Corporate Governance in Africa, 2016), available at www.carrotsandsticks.net, 23.

achieved international recognition. In addition, companies can turn to standards that are focused on single issues such as greenhouse gas emissions, climate change, or the impacts of business activity on forests.[2] It has been noted that distinctions can be made among normative, management, and reporting frameworks with respect to sustainability strategies and reporting. For example, the UN Global Compact principles and the OECD Guidelines provide normative frameworks to help companies shape their sustainability vision and management approach as well as to measure their impacts. ISO 26000 is an example of a management standard that organizations can use with respect to their corporate social responsibility strategies, processes, and activities. The reporting perspective is represented by the GRI's Sustainability Reporting Standards, which provide organizations with disclosure items and metrics that align with the most important international normative frameworks. Adding to the complexity is the emergence of sector-specific performance measurement and reporting frameworks, such as the GRESB for assessing environmental, social and governance (ESG) performance in the global commercial real estate sector. In addition, companies operating in specific sectors must take into account recommendations of sectoral trade associations, such as the guidance on reporting and communications discussed elsewhere in this publication provided by Finnish Textile and Fashion, the central organization for textile, clothing, and fashion companies in Finland.[3] Several of the more recognized sustainability reporting frameworks and instruments are briefly introduced in the following sections.

Global Reporting Initiative (GRI) Standards

The Global Reporting Initiative (GRI) (www.globalreporting.org) was founded in 1997 by the Coalition for Environmentally Responsible Economics (CERES) in Boston, Massachusetts, to develop a standardized sustainability reporting framework that would effectively capture and describe the sustainability activities that transpire in the economic,

---

[2] Id. at 25.

[3] *Finnish Textile and Fashion Corporate Responsibility Manual.* 55. Helsinki: Finnish Textile and Fashion.

environmental, and social aspects of organizational operations.[4] The goal of the GRI has been to serve as a multistakeholder-developed international independent organization that helps businesses, governments, and other organizations understand and communicate the impact of business on critical sustainability issues such as climate change, human rights, corruption, and many others. In so doing, reporting enterprises can make better decisions regarding the actions that should be taken toward a more sustainable economy and world. The Global Sustainability Standards Board (GSSB) issues and maintains the GRI reporting standards for organizations to use in their "sustainability reporting," described by the GSSB as "an organization's practice of reporting publicly on its economic, environmental, and/or social impacts, and hence its contributions—positive or negative—towards the goal of sustainable development."[5]

When it was formed, the GRI was one of the pioneers of sustainability reporting. Since then, the GRI has been a primary driver of transforming sustainability reporting from a niche practice to one now adopted by a growing majority of organizations. The GRI's standards are the world's most widely used with respect to sustainability reporting and disclosure and are available for use by public agencies, firms, and other organizations wishing to understand and communicate aspects of their economic, environmental, and social performance. The GRI's reporting standards are based on widely recognized international norms and normative frameworks on sustainability such as the UN Guiding Principles on Business and Human Rights, the International Labor Organization (ILO) Conventions, the UN Global Compact Ten Principles, and the Organisation for Economic Co-operation and Development (OECD) Guidelines for Multinational Enterprises.

In 1999, soon after its formation, the GRI entered into a partnership with the United Nations Environment Programme, and released the first two generations of official sustainability reporting guidelines in 2000

---

[4] Adapted from a description of the evolution of the Global Reporting Initiative included in Mink, K. 2012. *The Effects of Organizational Structure on Sustainability Report Compliance.* 12–13. Purdue University College of Technology Masters' Thesis. available athttp //docs.lib.purdue.edu/techmasters/62

[5] GRI 101: Foundation 2016 (Amsterdam: Stichting Global Reporting Initiative, 2016), 3.

and 2002, respectively. The GRI moved its headquarters to and released a third generation of guidelines (G3) in 2006 following a substantial amount of industry and professional feedback that, among other things, led to the inclusion of a set of sector supplements. The G3 guidelines laid down four fundamental principles for companies to follow when defining the content of their sustainability reports: materiality (i.e., the report should cover topics that reflect the company's significant economic, environmental, and social impacts), stakeholder inclusiveness (i.e., the report should identify the company's stakeholders and explain how the company has responded to their reasonable expectations and interests), sustainability context (i.e., performance should be explained in the wider context of sustainability), and completeness (i.e., the report should cover material topics and their boundaries, sufficient to reflect significant economic, environmental, and social impacts, and to enable stakeholders to assess organizational performance).

The fourth generation of guidelines (G4) was issued by the and was intended, at least in part, to address concerns that had been raised in some quarters regarding the sheer weight of the metrics involved in the previous reporting framework and represented an effort to return to certain core principles of reporting such as materiality. The GRI guidelines described in detail in another chapter of this publication, generally referred to as the "GRI Standards," are the latest version of the GRI's sustainability reporting framework that were published, following extensive consultation, in October 2016 and formally went into effect for reports and other materials published on or after July 1, 2018.[6] Reporting is required in three categories: economic (e.g., economic performance, indirect economic impacts, procurement practices, etc.); environmental (e.g., materials, energy, water, transport, environmental grievance mechanisms, etc.); and social, which includes labor practices and decent work (e.g.,

---

[6] The GRI Standards replaced the G4 guidelines; however, the GRI explained that the transition for organizations that had previously used the G4 guidelines should be smooth since the main content, concepts, and requirements did not change and the most significant changes occurred with respect to structure and format. For more information, see the "Transition to Standards" page on the GRI website and "From Guidelines to Standards: Implication of the GRI Transition" (BSR Sustainability Matters Webinar, December 2016).

employment, occupational health and safety, training and education, etc.), human rights (e.g., nondiscrimination, forced or compulsory labor, indigenous rights, etc.), society (e.g., local communities, etc.), and product responsibility (e.g., customer health and safety, product and service labeling, customer privacy, etc.). The GRI Standards include universal reporting principles, guidance on reporting contextual information about an organization, and its sustainability reporting practices and guidance on reporting how an organization manages a material reporting topic and each topic comes with its own specific requirements, recommendations, and guidance. The GRI is not a rating agency, does not monitor whether a particular organization has correctly applied its guidelines, and does not provide any certifications.

International Integrated Reporting Framework

The International Integrated Reporting Council or (IIRC; www.theiirc .org) is a global coalition of regulators, investors, companies, standard setters, the accounting profession, and nongovernment organizations (NGOs) dedicated to promoting communications about value creation as the next step in the evolution of corporate reporting.[7] The IIRC, which was founded in August 2010, released its International Integrated Reporting Framework in December 2013 as a guide that companies could use to describe how their governance structure creates value in the short, medium, and long term; supports decision making that takes into account risks and includes mechanisms for addressing ethical issues; exceeds legal requirements; and ensures that the culture, ethics, and values of the company are reflected in its use of and effects on the company's "capitals" (described to include financial, manufactured, intellectual, human, social and relationship, and natural (i.e., the environment and natural resources) forms of value) and stakeholder relationships.[8]

---

[7] Carrots and Sticks: Global Trends in Sustainability Reporting Regulation and Policy (KPMG International, the Global Research Initiative ("GRI"), the United Nations Environment Programme ("UNEP") and the Centre for Corporate Governance in Africa, 2016), available at www.carrotsandsticks.net, 25.

[8] P. DeSimone, Board Oversight of Sustainability Issues: A Study of the S & P 500 (IRRC Institute, March 2014), 7.

The International Integrated Reporting Council (IRRC) Framework was aimed primarily at producing information for long-term investors and providing companies with guiding principles and content elements that would govern the content of their integrated reports.[9] The executive summary to the framework explained that the drafters had taken a principles-based approach with the intent to strike an appropriate balance between flexibility and prescription that recognized the wide variation in individual circumstances of different organizations while enabling a sufficient degree of comparability across organizations to meet relevant information needs. According to the executive summary, the following guiding principles underpin the preparation of an integrated report, informing the content of the report and how information is presented[10]:

- *Strategic focus and future orientation*: An integrated report should provide insight into the organization's strategy, and how it relates to the organization's ability to create value in the short, medium, and long term, and to its use of and effects on the capitals
- *Connectivity of information*: An integrated report should show a holistic picture of the combination, interrelatedness and dependencies between the factors that affect the organization's ability to create value over time
- *Stakeholder relationships*: An integrated report should provide insight into the nature and quality of the organization's relationships with its key stakeholders, including how and to what extent the organization understands, takes into account and responds to their legitimate needs and interests
- *Materiality*: An integrated report should disclose information about matters that substantively affect the organization's ability to create value over the short, medium, and long term
- *Conciseness*: An integrated report should be concise

---

[9] The International < IR > Framework (International Integrated Reporting Council, December 2013).
[10] Id. at 5.

- *Reliability and completeness*: An integrated report should include all material matters, both positive and negative, in a balanced way and without material error
- *Consistency and comparability*: The information in an integrated report should be presented: (a) on a basis that is consistent over time; and (b) in a way that enables comparison with other organizations to the extent it is material to the organization's own ability to create value over time.

In addition, the executive summary to the framework explained that reports should include the following content elements, each of which are fundamentally linked to each other and are not mutually exclusive[11]:

- *Organizational overview and external environment*: What does the organization do and what are the circumstances under which it operates?
- *Governance*: How does the organization's governance structure support its ability to create value in the short, medium and long term?
- *Business model*: What is the organization's business model?
- *Risks and opportunities*: What are the specific risks and opportunities that affect the organization's ability to create value over the short, medium and long term, and how is the organization dealing with them?
- *Strategy and resource allocation*: Where does the organization want to go and how does it intend to get there?
- *Performance*: To what extent has the organization achieved its strategic objectives for the period and what are its outcomes in terms of effects on the capitals?
- *Outlook*: What challenges and uncertainties is the organization likely to encounter in pursuing its strategy, and what are the

---

[11] Id.

potential implications for its business model and future performance?

- *Basis of presentation*: How does the organization determine what matters to include in the integrated report and how are such matters quantified or evaluated?

Sustainability Accounting Standards Board

The Sustainability Accounting Standards Board (SASB) (www.sasb.org) is a U.S.-based independent standards-setting organization for sustainability accounting standards that was incorporated in July 2011 to meet the needs of investors by fostering high-quality disclosure of material sustainability information. The SASB has established industry-based sustainability standards for the recognition and disclosure of material environmental, social, and governance impacts by companies traded on U.S. exchanges.[12] The standards focus on known trends and uncertainties that are reasonably likely to affect the financial condition or operating performance of a company and therefore would be considered material under mandatory disclosure requirements, such as Regulation S-K applicable to disclosures made by U.S. reporting companies in the public filings with the Securities and Exchange Commission (SEC). The SASB is an ANSI accredited standards developer; however, it is not affiliated with the Financial Accounting Standards Board (FASB), the Governmental Accounting Standards Board (GASB), the International Accounting Standards Board (IASB), or any other accounting standards board. SASB standards do not include a scoring system, instead the focus is on providing companies with a standardized methodology that can be deployed when reporting sustainability performance through their regular regulatory reporting to the SEC on Forms 10 K and 10-Q (i.e., an "integrated reporting" approach as opposed to separate nonfinancial reports). SASB's standards enable comparison of peer performance and benchmarking

---

[12] Carrots and Sticks: Global Trends in Sustainability Reporting Regulation and Policy (KPMG International, the Global Research Initiative (GRI), the United Nations Environment Programme (UNEP) and the Centre for Corporate Governance in Africa, 2016), available at www.carrotsandsticks.net, 25.

within an industry and the SASB has gathered the support of Bloomberg LP and the Rockefeller Foundation.

The SASB publishes the SASB Implementation Guide for Companies that provides the structure and the key considerations for companies seeking to implement sustainability accounting standards within their existing business functions and processes. The Guide helps companies to select sustainability topics; assess the current state of disclosure and management embed SASB standards into financial reporting and management processes; support disclosure and management with internal control; and present information for disclosure. The SASB's online resource library also includes annual reports on the state of disclosure, industry briefs, and standards and guidance on stakeholder engagement. Companies should monitor CSR disclosures by their peers and the SASB library has examples of disclosures made by companies in annual reports filed with the SEC on Forms 10 K, 8 K, and so on. Companies can also follow the reporting practices of competitors by reviewing sustainability reported registered with the GRI.

The SASB is involved in establishing industry standards for sustainability disclosure and reporting and has explained that the decision regarding whether a particular sustainability topic warrants an industry standard are made on the basis of several factors including the potential to affect corporate value, investor interest, relevance across an industry, actionability by companies (i.e., whether individual companies are in a position to control or influence actions with respect to a particular topic and whether there is consensus among companies and investors that a disclosure topic is reasonably likely to constitute material information for most companies in the industry). As , the SASB had established and was currently maintaining provisional sustainability accounting standards for 79 industries across 11 sectors and companies should refer to the standards applicable to their business operations to identify and understand the relevant disclosure topics.[13]

---

[13] See Sustainability Accounting Standards Board, Disclosure Topics Tables (July 11, 2017).

International Standards of Accounting and Reporting

The Intergovernmental Working Group of Experts on International Standards of Accounting and Reporting (ISAR), which is hosted by the United Nations Conference on Trade and Development (UNCTAD), has issued a series of reports relating to nonfinancing reporting that provide guidance to companies on environmental accounting and reporting, corporate governance disclosure, and corporate responsibility reporting in annual reports. ISAR assists developing countries and economies in transition in the implementation of best practices for accounting and corporate governance with the goal of enhancing the investment climate in those countries and economies and promoting sustainable development.

British Standard on Sustainability Management, BS 8900

The British Standard on Sustainability Management, referred to as BS 8900, was first published in May 2006 by BSI (www.bsigroup.com) for use in independently auditing, verifying, and certifying an organization's sustainable development strategy and a fully revised version was issued in Part I of BS 8900 contains guidance on principles of sustainable development such as inclusivity, integrity, stewardship, and transparency and how those principles can be embedded in organizations. Part II of BS 8900 sets out the framework for assessing an organization's approach to sustainable development. The drafters of BS 8900 emphasized that it was not designed to duplicate existing management systems specifications, such as ISO 9001 or ISO 14001, but was intended to optimize the value of existing approaches. BS 8900 was developed for the consultants and managers responsible for sustainability within an organization, including the CEO and senior executives responsible for sustainability, compliance, corporate social responsibility, and environment.

European Union NonFinancial Reporting Directive

Directive 2014/95/EU on disclosure of nonfinancial and diversity information by certain large undertakings and groups was adopted by the and countries were required to transpose the rules stemming from the Directive into national law by December 2016, meaning that the prescribed nonfinancial information first appeared in the report prepared for the 2017 financial year.[14] The Directive applies to public-interest entities (PIEs) in the EU with more than 500 employees[15] and requires them to include in their management report (or in a separate report if the required information already appears in that report) a nonfinancial statement containing information on their policies, main risks, and outcomes related to, at a minimum, environmental matters, social and employee aspects, respect for human rights, anticorruption, and bribery issues. Companies are required to include a brief description of their business model, a description of their policies in relation to the nonfinancial matters and the outcome of these policies and a description of the principal risks relating to nonfinancial matters and how the company manages those risks. If a company does not pursue policies in relation to one or more of the nonfinancial matters listed previously, it must give a clear and reasoned explanation for not doing so; however, companies are allowed not to disclose commercially sensitive information under certain circumstances. In addition, the Directive requires PIEs listed on an EU regulated markets to provide information as part of their corporate governance statement on their diversity policy applied to their administrative, supervisory, and management bodies (e.g., age, gender, and educational and professional background).[16]

---

[14] Carrots and Sticks: Global Trends in Sustainability Reporting Regulation and Policy (KPMG International, the Global Research Initiative (GRI), the United Nations Environment Programme (UNEP) and the Centre for Corporate Governance in Africa, 2016), available at www.carrotsandsticks.net, 23.

[15] The definition of PIEs in the Directive covers listed companies, banks, insurance undertakings, and other companies that are so designated by Member States, and some of the Member States have extended the scope of coverage beyond that required in the Directive to include entities such hospitals and even municipalities. The European Commission estimated that the reporting requirements would initially apply to more than 6,000 entities across the EU.

[16] Disclosures regarding the diversity policy need to set out the objectives of the policy, how it was implemented, and the results. If a company does not have a diversity policy it needs to explain why.

When reporting, companies are allowed to refer to a number of different reporting standards including the Eco-Management and Audit Scheme and international reporting frameworks such as the GRI, the UN Global Compact, the UN Guiding Principles on Business and Human Rights, the OECD Guidelines for Multinational Enterprises, ISO 26000, and the ILO's Tripartite Declaration of Principles Concerning Multinational Enterprises and Social Policy.[17] In addition, in June 2017 the European Commission published its Guidelines on Nonfinancial Reporting (C 215/01) to help companies disclose environmental and social information. These guidelines are not mandatory and companies may decide to use international, European, or national guidelines according to their own characteristics or business environment. This is important given that country-specific implementations of the Directive are not uniform and companies conducting business across the EU will likely need to address and comply with multiple nonfinancial reporting frameworks including requirements that had been imposed prior to the adoption and implementation of the Directive.

Dow Jones Sustainability Indexes

The Dow Jones Sustainability Index includes the top 10 percent of the 2,500 largest companies in the S & P Global Broad Market Index based on their Sustainability Score as determined through the Corporate Sustainability Assessment, which takes into account performance vis-à-vis peers and media and stakeholder analysis. Scoring is based on industry-specific criteria considered by investors to be material, with equal balance being given to economic, social, and environmental indicators. The Index has been consistently recognized as being among the most credible sustainability rating protocols.

---

[17] For further information on reporting of nonfinancial information in the EU pursuant to the Directive, see https://globalreporting.org/information/policy/Pages/EUpolicy.aspx and https://ec.europa.eu/info/business-economy-euro/company-reporting-and-auditing/company-reporting/non-financial-reporting_en

Business and SDGs: SDG Compass and the 12.6 Tracker

The GRI, the UN Global Compact, and the World Business Council for Sustainable Development collaborated to create the SDG Compass as a guide to help businesses understand and contribute to the Sustainable Development Goals (SDGs) adopted in September 2015 by the 2030 Agenda for Sustainable Development. The 12.6 Tracker, a collaborative effort between the GRI and Tata Consultancy Services, is a database that governments can use to understand the status of sustainability reporting in their countries and track progress toward SDG Goal 12.6, which encourages companies to integrate sustainability information into their reporting cycles.[18]

United Nations Global Compact

The United Nations Global Compact (UNGC) has been described as the largest policy initiative for businesses that are committed to aligning their operations and strategies with ten universally accepted principles in the areas of human rights, labor, environment, and anticorruption derived from UN Declarations and Conventions.[19] UNGC signatories are required to issue an annual Communication on Progress (COP), which is a public disclosure to their stakeholders on progress made in implementing the ten principles. Failure to issue a COP can result in a signatory's status being changed to "noncommunicating" and can eventually lead to expulsion.[20]

---

[18] Carrots and Sticks: Global Trends in Sustainability Reporting Regulation and Policy (KPMG International, the Global Research Initiative (GRI), the United Nations Environment Programme (UNEP) and the Centre for Corporate Governance in Africa, 2016), available at www.carrotsandsticks.net, 24.

[19] Carrots and Sticks: Global Trends in Sustainability Reporting Regulation and Policy (KPMG International, the Global Research Initiative (GRI), the United Nations Environment Programme (UNEP) and the Centre for Corporate Governance in Africa, 2016), available at www.carrotsandsticks.net, 25.

[20] Id. at 26.

OECD Guidelines for Multinational Enterprises

The OECD Guidelines provide recommendations for responsible business conduct in areas such as employment and industrial relations, human rights, environment, information disclosure, combating bribery, consumer interests, science and technology, competition, and taxation.[21]

ISO 26000

ISO 26000:2010 provides guidance to all types of organizations, regardless of their size or location, on concepts, terms, and definitions related to social responsibility; the background, trends, and characteristics of social responsibility; principles and practices relating to social responsibility; the core subjects and issues of social responsibility; integrating, implementing, and promoting socially responsible behavior throughout the organization and, through its policies and practices, within its sphere of influence; identifying and engaging with stakeholders; and communicating commitments, performance, and other information related to social responsibility. ISO 26000:2010 is intended to assist organizations in contributing to sustainable development; however, it is not a management system standard and is not intended or appropriate for certification purposes or regulatory or contractual use.[22] Although ISO 26000:2010 is primarily a guidance standard on how business and organizations can operate in a socially responsible way, it does call on organizations to, at appropriate intervals, report about its performance on social responsibility to the stakeholders affected, which would mean reporting on each of the "core subjects" defined and described in ISO 26000:2010: organizational governance; human rights; labor practices; the environment; fair

---

[21] Id.

[22] See International Organization for Standardization, ISO 26000 Guidance on Social Responsibility: Discovering ISO 26000 (2014) and *Handbook for Implementers of ISO 26000, Global Guidance Standard on Social Responsibility by Small and Medium Sized Businesses* (Middlebury VT: ECOLOGIA, 2011).

operating practices; consumer issues; and community involvement and development.[23]

CDP (Carbon Disclosure Project)

The CDP, formerly the Carbon Disclosure Project (CDP) (www.cdp .net), provides a global reporting system that collects information from the world's largest organizations on their climate change risks, opportunities, strategies, and performance, and the way in which they consume and affect natural resources including water and forests. The CDP has built the most comprehensive collection of self-reported environmental data in the world and has been praised as a catalyst for driving thousands of companies and cities across the world's largest economies to measure and disclose their greenhouse gas emissions, climate change risk, and water strategies.[24] The CDP operates through various programs focusing on relevant areas such as climate change, water, supply chain, forests, and cities, and has spearheaded a carbon action initiative to encourage acceleration of carbon reduction in high-emitting industries and implementation of emissions reducing projects that generate positive return on investment. CDP scores companies and other types of reporting organizations (e.g., cities, government agencies, NGOs, and supply chains) on disclosure and performance and has recognized top scoring organizations in the Carbon Disclosure Leadership Index. Backed by all of the largest institutional investors around the world, the CDOP has been consistently recognized as being among the world's most credible sustainability rating protocols.

Greenhouse Gas Protocol (GHG Protocol) Corporate Standard

The Greenhouse Gas Protocol (GHG Protocol) (www.ghgprotocol.org), a decade-long partnership between the World Resources Institute (WRI)

---

[23] Carrots and Sticks: Global Trends in Sustainability Reporting Regulation and Policy (KPMG International, the Global Research Initiative (GRI), the United Nations Environment Programme (UNEP) and the Centre for Corporate Governance in Africa, 2016), available at www.carrotsandsticks.net, 26.
[24] Id.

and the World Business Council for Sustainable Development (WBCSD), is the most widely used international accounting tool for government and business leaders to understand, quantify, and manage greenhouse gas emissions. The GHG Protocol provides the accounting framework for nearly every GHG standard and program in the world—from the International Standards Organization to The Climate Registry—as well as hundreds of GHG inventories prepared by individual companies.[25] The GHG Protocol includes several different standards suitable for use by companies, organizations, communities, cities, and countries. For example, the GHG Protocol Corporate Accounting and Reporting Standard was intended to provide requirements and guidance for companies and other organizations, such as NGOs, government agencies, and universities that are preparing a corporate-level GHG emissions inventory. The Product Standard can be used to understand the full lifecycle emissions of a product and focus efforts on the greatest GHG reduction opportunities, thus making a significant contribution toward the design and commercialization of more sustainable products. The Corporate Value Chain (Scope 3) Standard allows companies to assess their entire value chain emissions impact and identify where to focus their resources on reduction activities.[26]

ILO Tripartite Declaration of Principles Concerning Multinational Enterprises and Social Policy

The ILO Tripartite Declaration of Principles Concerning Multinational Enterprises and Social Policy are intended to serve as guidelines to multinational enterprises, governments, and employers' and workers' organizations in such areas as employment, training, conditions of work and life, and industrial relations. The ILO has also promulgated certain baseline standards for labor, referred to as the Core Labor Standards, which have become widely accepted as customary international law and include freedom of association and the right to collective bargaining; the elimination

---

[25] Id.

[26] http://ghgprotocol.org/standards

of forced and compulsory labor; the abolition of child labor; and the elimination of discrimination in the workplace.[27]

UN Guiding Principles on Business and Human Rights

The "Guiding Principles on Business and Human Rights: Implementing the United Nations 'Protect, Respect and Remedy' Framework" were endorsed by the and include guiding principles on, among other things, the role of business enterprises as specialized organs of society performing specialized functions and their duties to comply with all applicable laws and to respect human rights. The Guiding Principles call on business enterprises to communicate on how they address their human rights impacts, with communications ranging from informal engagement with affected stakeholders to formal public reporting, with formal reporting required in those instances where operations or operating contexts pose risks of severe human rights impacts. The Guiding Principles also require states to encourage, or where appropriate require, such communications as important in fostering respect for human rights by business enterprises.[28] The Guiding Principles call on companies to ensure that their communications are in a form and frequency that reflect the company's human rights impacts and are accessible to its intended audiences; provide information that is sufficient to evaluate the adequacy of the company's response to the particular human rights impact involved; and in turn not pose risks to affected stakeholders, personnel or to legitimate requirements of commercial confidentiality.

PRI Reporting Framework

The United Nations-supported Principles for Responsible Investment (PRI) Initiative is an international network of investors working together to put the six Principles for Responsible Investment into practice

---

[27] Carrots and Sticks: Global Trends in Sustainability Reporting Regulation and Policy (KPMG International, the Global Research Initiative (GRI), the United Nations Environment Programme (UNEP) and the Centre for Corporate Governance in Africa, 2016), available at www.carrotsandsticks.net, 26.
[28] Id. at 27.

including a menu of possible actions for incorporating environmental, social, and governance issues into investment practices across asset classes. Signatories to the PRI are required to publicly report and disclose on various mandatory indicators.[29]

Climate Disclosure Standards Board

The Climate Change Reporting Framework, which was launched in 2010 by the Climate Disclosure Standards Board (CDSB), an international consortium of business and environmental NGOs, provides a standards-ready tool for companies to disclose climate change-related information in mainstream financial reports that is based on relevant provisions of existing standards and practices, including the Greenhouse Gas Protocol and International Financial Reporting Standards, and regulatory and voluntary reporting and carbon trading rules.[30] According to the CDSB, the goal is to offer companies a reporting framework for reporting environmental information with the same rigor as financial information, thus supporting the efforts of companies to provide investors with decision-useful environmental information in their corporate reports.

The objectives of the CDSB Framework are to help companies translate their sustainability information into business impacts and long-term value; provide clear, concise, and consistent information to investors, connecting the organization's environmental performance to its overall strategy, performance, and prospects; enable and encourage informed investor decision making on the allocation of financial capital; and add value to an organization's existing mainstream report, while minimizing the reporting burden and simplifying the reporting process. The Framework also supports compliance with regulatory reporting requirements with current and emerging requirements for environmental reporting, (e.g., the EU Nonfinancial Reporting Directive); aligns and complements the objectives of financial reporting by providing environmental

---

[29] Id.
[30] Id.

information that is connected with financial information; aligns with the recommendations of the Task Force on Climate-related Financial Disclosures; builds on the most widely used reporting approaches, such as CDP, GRI, SASB, and IFRS; encourages standardization of environmental information reporting; supports the rigor that is appropriate for information provided to investors; helps prepare assurable reports; and the CDSB Framework is complementary to the Natural Capital Protocol.[31]

---

[31] https://cdsb.net/what-we-do/reporting-frameworks/environmental-information-natural-capital

CHAPTER 4

Global Reporting Initiative ("GRI") Standards

It is generally acknowledged that the standards developed by the Global Reporting Initiative (GRI) (www.globalreporting.org) are the world's most widely used with respect to sustainability reporting and disclosure. The latest version of the GRI's sustainability reporting framework, generally referred to as the "GRI Standards," were published, following extensive consultation, in October 2016 and formally went into effect for reports and other materials published on or after July 1, 2018.[1] The Global Sustainability Standards Board (GSSB) issues and maintains the GRI Standards for organizations to use in their "sustainability reporting," described by the GSSB as "an organization's practice of reporting publicly on its economic, environmental, and/or social impacts, and hence its contributions—positive or negative—towards the goal of sustainable development."[2] The GSSB has explained:

> Through this process, an organization identifies its significant impacts on the economy, the environment, and/or society and discloses them in accordance with a globally-accepted standard. The GRI Standards create a common language for organizations

---

[1] The GRI Standards replaced the G4 guidelines; however, the GRI explained that the transition for organizations that had previously used the G4 guidelines should be smooth since the main content, concepts, and requirements did not change and the most significant changes occurred with respect to structure and format. For more information, see the "Transition to Standards" page on the GRI website and "From Guidelines to Standards: Implication of the GRI Transition" (BSR Sustainability Matters Webinar, December 2016).

[2] GRI 101: Foundation 2016 (Amsterdam: Stichting Global Reporting Initiative, 2016), 3.

and stakeholders, with which the economic, environmental, and social impacts of organizations can be communicated and understood. The Standards are designed to enhance the global comparability and quality of information on these impacts, thereby enabling greater transparency and accountability of organizations.[3]

Each of the GRI Standards includes requirements (i.e., mandatory instructions presented in bold font and indicated with the word "shall"); recommendations (i.e., a particular course of action which is encouraged, but not required, and indicated with the word "should"); and guidance (i.e., background information, explanations and examples). The GRI Standards are divided into four Series[4]:

100 Series: The 100 Series includes three universal Standards:

- GRI 101: Foundation is the starting point for using the set of GRI Standards. GRI 101 sets out the Reporting Principles for defining report content and quality. It includes the requirements for preparing a sustainability report in accordance with the GRI Standards and describes how the GRI Standards can be used and referenced. GRI 101 also includes the specific claims that are required for organizations preparing a sustainability report in accordance with the Standards, and for those using selected GRI Standards to report specific information.
- GRI 102: General Disclosures provide guidance on reporting contextual information about an organization and its sustainability reporting practices. This includes information about an organization's profile, strategy, ethics and integrity, governance, stakeholder engagement practices, and reporting process.

---

[3] Id.

[4] Id. at 4.

- GRI 103: Management Approach is used to report information about how an organization manages a material topic. It is designed to be used for each material topic in a sustainability report, including those covered by the topic-specific GRI Standards (Series 200, 300, and 400) and other material topics.

Topic-specific Standards: The GRI Standards include three series of topic-specific standards: the 200 series for economic topics; the 300 series for environmental topics, and the 400 series for social topics. These topic-specific standards can be used by organizations to report information on their impacts relating to a wide range of economic, environmental, and social topics (e.g., indirect economic impacts, water, or employment).[5]

When organizations set out to prepare a sustainability report in accordance with the GRI Standards, they begin by applying the reporting principles for defining report content from "GRI 101: Foundation" to identify its material economic, environmental, and/or social topics. These material topics determine which topic-specific Standards the organization uses to prepare its sustainability report.

GRI 101 (Foundation)

GRI 101, referred to as the "Foundation," is intended to be the starting point for an organization to use the GRI Standards to report about its economic, environmental, and/or social impacts.[6] There are three sections to GRI 101:

---

[5] Each topic-specific Standard follows a standardized format that begins with an overview of the disclosures in the Standard, continues with the specific management approach disclosures for the Standard, and then moves to the reporting requirements, recommendations and/or guidance associated with each of the topic-specific disclosures for the Standard. For example, GRI 401 (Employment) provides that reporting organizations must report its management approach for employment using GRI 103 (Management Approach) and then includes three topic-specific disclosures based on the Standard number: 401-1 New employee hires and employee turnover; 401-2 Benefits provided to full-time employees that are not provided to temporary or part-time employees; and 401-3 Parental leave.
[6] The information in this section on GRI 101 is adapted from GRI 101: Foundation 2016 (Amsterdam: Stichting Global Reporting Initiative, 2016), which is available for download at www.globalreporting.org.

- Section 1 presents the "reporting principles" for defining report content and report quality and must be used by organizations to help them decide what information to include in a sustainability report and how to ensure the quality of the information.
- Section 2 explains the basic process for using the GRI Standards for sustainability reporting and includes fundamental requirements for applying the reporting principles, and for identifying and reporting on material topics.
- Section 3 sets out ways that the GRI Standards can be used and the specific claims, or statements of use, which are required for organizations using the GRI Standards.

The reporting principles are considered to be fundamental to achieving high-quality sustainability reporting and are required to be applied by any organization seeking to claim that its sustainability report has been prepared in accordance with the GRI Standards. The reporting principles, which are presented with guidance that includes tests that organizations can reference to gauge compliance with a particular principle, are divided into two groups, the first one of which includes the following principles for defining report content following consideration of the organization's activities, impacts, and the substantive expectations and interests of its stakeholders:

- *Stakeholder Inclusiveness*: The reporting organization shall identify its stakeholders and explain how it has responded to their reasonable expectations and interests.
- *Sustainability Context*: The report shall present the reporting organization's performance in the wider context of sustainability.
- *Materiality*: The report shall cover topics that reflect the reporting organization's significant economic, environmental, and social impacts; or substantively influence the assessments and decisions of stakeholders.

- *Completeness:* The report shall include coverage of material topics and their boundaries,[7] sufficient to reflect significant economic, environmental, and social impacts, and to enable stakeholders to assess the reporting organization's performance in the reporting period.[8]

The second group of reporting principles includes the following principles for defining and ensuring report quality, including the proper presentation of information:

- *Accuracy:* The reported information shall be sufficiently accurate and detailed for stakeholders to assess the reporting organization's performance.
- *Balance:* The reported information shall reflect positive and negative aspects of the reporting organization's performance to enable a reasoned assessment of overall performance.
- *Clarity:* The reporting organization shall make information available in a manner that is understandable and accessible to stakeholders using that information.
- *Comparability:* The reporting organization shall select, compile, and report information consistently. The reported information shall be presented in a manner that enables stakeholders to

---

[7] A topic "boundary" is a description of where the impacts occur for a material topic, and the organization's involvement with those impacts. Organizations might be involved with impacts either through their own activities or as a result of their business relationships with other entities. GRI 101: Foundation 2016 (Amsterdam: Stichting Global Reporting Initiative, 2016), 12.

[8] Many organizations simply organize their sustainability reports by reference to the particular Standards that are materially applicable to their operations and thus necessary in order to provide readers with a picture of the organization's significant economic, environmental, and/or social impacts. In some cases, however, organizations will combine reporting on several different Standards into a broader material topic (e.g., several of the Standards in Series 400 may be grouped together and reported as "Human Rights" or indirect impacts of the organization's activities, which are covered in Series 200, and impacts of those activities on local communities, which are covered in Series 400, may be reported together as "Community Impact and Development").

analyze changes in the organization's performance over time, and
that could support analysis relative to other organizations.

- *Reliability*: The reporting organization shall gather, record,
compile, analyze, and report information and processes used in
the preparation of the report in a way that they can be subject to
examination, and that establishes the quality and materiality of
the information.
- *Timeliness*: The reporting organization shall report on a regular
schedule so that information is available in time for stakeholders
to make informed decisions.

Section 2 of GRI 101 sets out the following basic requirements for
organizations wishing to use the GRI Standards for their sustainability
reporting[9]:

- *Applying the Reporting Principles*: The reporting organization shall
apply all reporting principles from Section 1 to define report
content and quality.
- *Reporting General Disclosures*: The reporting organization
shall report the required disclosures from GRI 102: General
Disclosures (see as follows).
- *Identifying Material Topics and Their Boundaries*: The reporting
organization shall identify its material topics using the reporting
principles for defining report content. The reporting organization
should consult the GRI Sector Disclosures that relate to its sector,
if available, to assist with identifying its material topics. In addition, the reporting organization shall identify the boundary for
each material topic.
- *Reporting on Material Topics*: For each material topic, the reporting organization shall report the management approach disclosures for that topic, using GRI 103: Management Approach

---

[9] GRI 101: Foundation 2016 (Amsterdam: Global Reporting Initiative, 2016),
17–20.

(see the following); and either (1) shall report the topic-specific disclosures in the corresponding GRI Standard, if the material topic is covered by an existing GRI Standard (i.e., Series 200, 300, and 400), or (2) should report other appropriate disclosures, if the material topic is not covered by an existing GRI Standard.

- *Presenting Information*: If the reporting organization reports a required disclosure using a reference to another source where the information is located, the organization shall ensure that the reference includes the specific location of the required disclosure and that the referenced information is publicly available and readily accessible.

- *Compiling and Presenting Information in the Report*: When preparing a sustainability report, the reporting organization should: present information for the current reporting period and at least two previous periods as well as future short and medium-term targets if they have been established; compile and report information using generally accepted international metrics (such as kilograms or liters) and standard conversion factors, and explain the basis of measurement/calculation where not otherwise apparent; provide absolute data and explanatory notes when using ratios or normalized data; and define a consistent reporting period for issuing a report.

Section 3 of GRI 101 sets out the conditions that must be satisfied by an organization in order for it to properly claim its sustainability report has been prepared in accordance with the GRI Standards.[10] Organizations can choose between two options for preparing a sustainability report in accordance with the GRI Standards. The first option, referred to as "Core," indicates that a report contains the minimum information needed to understand the nature of the organization, its material topics, and related impacts and how they are managed. The second option, referred to as "Comprehensive," builds on the Core option by requiring additional disclosures on the organization's strategy, ethics and integrity,

---

[10] Id. at 21–26.

and governance. In addition, an organization using the Comprehensive option must report more extensively on its impacts by reporting all of the topic-specific disclosures for each material topic covered by the GRI Standards (i.e., Series 200, 300, and 400).[11] Specific guidelines in Section 3 include the following[12]:

- To claim that a sustainability report has been prepared in accordance with the GRI Standards, the reporting organization must meet all criteria for the respective option (Core or Comprehensive) from Table 4.1 in GRI 101.[13]

- If, in exceptional cases, an organization preparing a sustainability report in accordance with the GRI Standards cannot report a required disclosure, the organization must provide in the report a reason for omission that describes the specific information that has been omitted; and specifies one of several reasons for omission recognized in GRI 101, including the required explanation for that reason.[14]

- If the reporting organization uses selected GRI Standards, or parts of their content, to report specific information, but has not met the afore-referenced criteria to prepare a report in accordance with the GRI Standards, the organization: shall include in any published material with disclosures based on the GRI Standards a statement that (i) contains the following text: "This material references [title and publication year of the Standard]," for each Standard used; and (ii) indicates which specific content from the Standard has been applied, if the Standard has not been used in full; shall comply with all reporting requirements that correspond to the disclosures reported; shall notify GRI of the

---

[11] Id. at 21.

[12] Id. at 22–26.

[13] Table 4.1 of GRI 101 lists the criteria to claim a report has been prepared in accordance with either the Core or Comprehensive option. Id. at 23.

[14] Table 4.2 of GRI 101 lists four acceptable reasons for omission (i.e., "not applicable," "confidentiality constraints", "specific legal prohibitions" and "information unavailable") and described the required explanation that must be included in the sustainability report for each type of omission. Id. at 24.

use of the Standards; should apply the Reporting Principles for defining report quality from Section 1 of GRI 101 (as mentioned earlier); and should report its management approach by applying GRI 103: Management Approach (see the following) together with any topic-specific Standard (i.e., Series 200, 300, or 400) used.

- The reporting organization shall notify GRI of its use of the GRI Standards, and the claim it has made in the report or published material, by either sending a copy to GRI at standards@global-reporting.org; or registering the report or published material at www.globalreporting.org/standards.

GRI 102 (General Disclosures)

GRI 102 includes the "general disclosures" that organizations are expected to use to report contextual information about their activities and operations and their sustainability reporting practices.[15] This includes information about an organization's profile, strategy, ethics and integrity, governance, stakeholder engagement practices, and reporting process. Contextual information regarding an organization (e.g., its size, geographic location, and activities) is important to assist stakeholders in understanding the nature of the organization and its economic, environmental, and social impacts. Specific topics within the overall framework for these general disclosures include the following:

Organizational Profile

- Name of the organization
- Activities, brands, products, and services
- Location of headquarters
- Location of operations
- Ownership and legal form
- Markets served

---

[15] GRI 102: General Disclosures 2016 (Amsterdam: Stichting Global Reporting Initiative, 2016). GRI 102 is available for download at www.globalreporting.org.

- Scale of the organization
- Information on employees and other workers
- Supply chain
- Significant changes to the organization and its supply chain
- Precautionary Principle or approach
- External initiatives
- Membership of associations

Strategy

- Statement from senior decision maker
- Key impacts, risks, and opportunities

Ethics and Integrity

- Values, principles, standards, and norms of behavior
- Mechanisms for advice and concerns about ethics

Governance

- Governance structure
- Delegating authority
- Executive-level responsibility for economic, environmental, and social topics
- Consulting stakeholders on economic, environmental, and social topics
- Composition of the highest governance body and its committees
- Chair of the highest governance body
- Nominating and selecting the highest governance body
- Conflicts of interest
- Role of highest governance body in setting purpose, values, and strategy
- Collective knowledge of highest governance body
- Evaluating the highest governance body's performance
- Identifying and managing economic, environmental, and social impacts

- Effectiveness of risk management processes
- Review of economic, environmental, and social topics
- Highest governance body's role in sustainability reporting
- Communicating critical concerns
- Nature and total number of critical concerns
- Remuneration policies
- Process for determining remuneration
- Stakeholders' involvement in remuneration
- Annual total compensation ratio
- Percentage increase in annual total compensation ratio

Stakeholder Engagement

- List of stakeholder groups
- Collective bargaining agreements
- Identifying and selecting stakeholders
- Approach to stakeholder engagement
- Key topics and concerns raised

Reporting Practice

- Entities included in the consolidated financial statements
- Defining report content and topic
- Boundaries
- List of material topics
- Restatements of information
- Changes in reporting
- Reporting period
- Date of most recent report
- Reporting cycle
- Contact point for questions regarding the report
- Claims of reporting in accordance with the GRI Standards
- GRI content index
- External assurance.

GRI 103 ("Management Approach")

GRI 103, referred to as the "Management Approach," sets out reporting requirements about the approach an organization uses to manage a material topic.[16] Disclosures relating to the management approach enable organizations to explain how they manage the economic, environmental, and social impacts related to their specific material topics by providing readers with narrative information about how the organization identifies, analyzes, and responds to its actual and potential impacts. Importantly, the disclosures about the organization's management approach provide context for the information reported using topic-specific Standards in Series 200,300, and 400.

An organization preparing a report in accordance with the GRI Standards is required to report its management approach for each material topic using GRI 103 and this requires an explanation of the material topic and its boundary, the management approach used for the topic and its components and an evaluation of the management approach. Topic-specific Standards can also contain additional reporting requirements, reporting recommendations, and/ or guidance for reporting management approach information about the topic in question. Reporting requirements come in the form of "disclosures" for each topic-specific Standard. For example, the Disclosure 401–1 in GRI 401 ("Employment") relates to "new employee hires and employee turnover" and requires reporting organizations to report both the total number and rate of new employee hires during the reporting period by age group, gender, and region *and* the total number and rate of employee turnover during the reporting period by age group, gender, and region. The purpose and context of these quantitative measures is to assess the organization's strategy and ability to attract diverse, qualified employees and the

---

[16] GRI 103: Management Approach 2016 (Amsterdam: Stichting Global Reporting Initiative, 2016). GRI 103 is available for download at www.globalreporting. org.

degree to which there may be uncertainty and dissatisfaction among employees.[17]

GRI 200 Series (Economic Topics)

The 200 series of the GRI Standards include topic-specific Standards used to report information on an organization's material impacts related to the following *economic* topics[18]:

- 201: Economic Performance
- 202: Market Presence
- 203: Indirect Economic Impacts
- 204: Procurement Practices
- 205: Anti-Corruption
- 206: Anti-Competitive Behavior

---

[17] When complying with the specific GRI disclosure and reporting requirements, organizations can also include other performance measures such as the "fitness metrics" recommended in the Future-Fit Business Benchmark. The Benchmark calls for organizations to apply a variety of fitness measures with respect to their own employees and employees working for core suppliers including the proportion of employees who are covered by well-functioning health programs that seek to safeguard both physical and mental well-being; the proportion of employees who are paid at least a living wage; the proportion of employees who have formal employment contracts that protect their rights to collective bargaining, fair working hours and parental leave; the proportion of employees who are covered by nondiscrimination policies and well-functioning programs that monitor, identify, and eliminate discriminatory practices; and the proportion of employees who have ready access to well-functioning concerns mechanisms capable of addressing any issues quickly, fairly and transparently. For further information on the fitness measures used in Future-Fit Business Benchmark, see "Future-Fit Business Benchmark: Key Fitness Indicators (KFIs) Calculations and Aggregation Methodologies" available at FutureFitBusiness.org. See also the discussion of the Future-Fit Business Benchmark in A. Gutterman, Strategic Planning for Sustainability (Oakland, CA: Sustainable Entrepreneurship Project, 2019) available at www.seproject.org.

[18] Each of the Standards in the GRI 200 Series is available for download at www.globalreporting.org.

GRI 300 Series ("Environmental Topics")

The 300 series of the GRI Standards include topic-specific Standards used to report information on an organization's material impacts related to the following *environmental* topics[19]:

- 301: Materials
- 302: Energy
- 303: Water
- 304: Biodiversity
- 305: Emissions
- 306: Effluents and Waste
- 307: Environmental Compliance
- 308: Supplier Environmental Assessment

GRI 400 Series ("Social Topics")

The 400 series of the GRI Standards include topic-specific Standards used to report information on an organization's material impacts related to the following *social* topics[20]:

- 401: Employment
- 402: Labor/Management Relations
- 403: Occupational Health and Safety
- 404: Training and Education
- 405: Diversity and Equal Opportunity
- 406: Non-Discrimination
- 407: Freedom of Association and Collective Bargaining
- 408: Child Labor
- 409: Forced or Compulsory Labor
- 410: Security Practices
- 411: Rights of Indigenous Peoples

---

[19] Each of the Standards in the GRI 300 Series is available for download at www.globalreporting.org.

[20] Each of the Standards in the GRI 400 Series is available for download at www.globalreporting.org.

- 412: Human Rights Assessment
- 413: Local Communities
- 414: Supplier Social Assessment
- 415: Public Policy
- 416: Customer Health and Safety
- 417: Marketing and Labeling
- 418: Customer Privacy
- 419: Socioeconomic Compliance

CHAPTER 5

SDG-Related Reporting

Delivery of the 17 Sustainable Development Goals (SDGs) in the 2030 Agenda for Sustainable Development should be important to businesses that realize that they will not be able to achieve sustainable success in a world of poverty, inequality, unrest, and environmental stress. As such, companies should contribute to the SDGs by upholding recognized standards and principles on human rights, labor, the environment, and anticorruption and transparently reporting on their SDG-related priorities and efforts to investors and other stakeholders.[1] report prepared and issued jointly by the Global Report Initiative, Principles for Responsible Investment and United Nations Global Compact, the argument was persuasively made that SDG reporting matters to both businesses and investors, which means that businesses should integrate SDG-related considerations into their business strategies and processes and existing reporting processes and engage in dialogue with their investor stakeholders to understand their needs and expectations on SDG reporting and how the reports will be utilized.[2] Some of the specific benefits to businesses from a global effort to make advances in business reporting on the SDGs include:

- Solidifying a common language for reporting a business's, and consequently investors', contribution to the SDGs, streamlining the reporting burden on sustainability issues;

---

[1] Integrating the SDGs into Corporate Reporting: A Practical Guide (Global Reporting Initiative, Principles for Responsible Investment and United Nations Global Compact, 2018), 4.

[2] In Focus: Addressing Investors Needs in Business Reporting on the SDGs (Global Reporting Initiative, Principles for Responsible Investment and United Nations Global Compact, 2018).

- Sparking collaboration along the investment chain to direct funds to more sustainable business practices, thereby incentivizing businesses to align core business activities with the SDGs;
- Helping unlock potential business opportunities, both by addressing risks to people and the environment and by developing new beneficial products, services and investments, while mitigating business risks related to the SDGs;
- Helping define a shared purpose between companies and investors about expected impact performance and commitment to support it.

At the level of a specific company, SDG reporting can serve as a valuable strategic tool for engaging stakeholders, supporting sustainable decision-making processes at all levels within a company, shaping business strategy, guiding innovation and driving better performance, and value creation and opening up new sources of capital.[3] In fact, the report referred to earlier also noted that research had shown that responsible business practices attracted sustainable finance, thus ensuring a virtuous cycle in the flow of goods, services, and capital that benefits other stakeholders and the natural environment. All of this is obviously important for businesses of all sizes; however, for sustainable entrepreneurs seeking capital for their business models, it reinforces the need for them to understand the needs, expectations, and investment criteria of impact and other investors who have elected to focus on new businesses interested in addressing specific environmental and social issues and problems.

As for investors, corporate SDG reporting can provide the following benefits:

- Obtaining additional insights to make better informed investment decisions that secure stable returns in line with fiduciary duty
- Representing their values or the values of their stakeholders

---

[3] Integrating the SDGs into Corporate Reporting: A Practical Guide (Global Reporting Initiative, Principles for Responsible Investment and United Nations Global Compact, 2018), 4.

- Offering sustainable and inclusive financial products that differentiate them in the market
- Understanding and improving their own SDG impact across their
portfolios
- Exploring new business models, markets, systems, and platforms
(e g., artificial intelligence or blockchain technologies) that would
support the increased availability and reliability of SDG-related
data
- Identifying and promoting innovative financing mechanisms
(e.g., SDG-related reporting could support the issuance of bonds
for projects that aim to create a positive contribution related to
the SDGs
- Meeting the requirements of national policies and investment
strategies that incorporate the SDGs, which is particularly relevant to state-owned investment institutions

SDG-related reporting also helps investors make informed investment decisions and direct their capital toward projects with positive real-
world impact. In addition, collecting further information on business
efforts relative to the SDGs is a valuable risk management tool for investors. For example, the costs from environment or climate-related events
will come back into investors' portfolios as insurance premiums, taxes,
inflated input prices, and physical cost associated with disasters, social
concerns, such as poverty and inequality, can lead to societal and political
unrest and instability that could reduce future cash flows and dividends.
Finally, investors have their own set of stakeholders, including pension
funds and other institutional investors as well as wealthy individuals looking to make an impact through their own investment activities, and it is
becoming increasingly important for them to demonstrate that sustainability, as demonstrated by requiring SDG-related reporting form their
portfolio companies, is part of their strategy.

There is no formal disclosure framework that has been specifically
developed relating to business reporting on the SDGs; however, reference

can and should be made to several useful and evolving guidance documents and related tools[4]:

- The SDG Compass, developed by the UN Global Compact, Global Reporting Initiative (GRI), and the World Business Council for Sustainable Development (WBCSD), includes preliminary information on the SDGs for business.
- The value driver model, developed by the Principles for Responsible Investment (PRI) and the UN Global Compact, uses key business metrics to determine and illustrate how corporate sustainability activities contribute to overall performance, and this tool can be used by companies to assess the financial impact of their sustainability strategies and communicate that impact clearly and effectively to investors.
- The 2017 "An Analysis of Goals and Targets," developed by GRI and the UN Global Compact, contains qualitative and quantitative disclosures from globally established reporting frameworks that can be used by business to measure and report on their impact and contribution to the SDG targets.
- *Integrating the SDGs into Corporate Reporting: A Practical Guide*, developed by the GRI, PRI, and the UN Global Compact, can be used by companies alongside the analysis to prioritize the SDGs, set business objectives, improve SDG-related performance, and disclose material information on outputs, outcomes, impacts, and contributions to the SDGs.

Integrating the SDGs into Corporate Reporting: A Practical Guide (SDG Reporting Guide) was developed by the Global Reporting Initiative (GRI), the Principles for Responsible Investment (PRI), and the United Nations Global Compact and first released in 2018 as a resource for companies to use in prioritizing the SDGs, setting business objectives, improving SDG-related performance and disclosing material information

---

[4] Recommendations adapted from In Focus: Addressing Investors Needs in Business Reporting on the SDGs (Global Reporting Initiative, Principles for Responsible Investment and United Nations Global Compact, 2018), 9.

on outputs, outcomes, impacts, and contributions to the SDGs. According to the SDG Reporting Guide, companies should follow a three-step process to embed the SDGs in existing businesses and reporting processes: principled prioritization of impacts and identification of SDGs for a company to act and report on, which involves understanding the SDGs and their targets, conducting principled prioritization of SDG targets and defining the company's SDG-related report content; setting of business objectives, selection of disclosures, and collection and analysis of data regarding performance; and reporting on the SDGs taking into account good practice and users' information needs and implementing changes to improve SDG performance.[5]

Understanding the SDGs and Associated Targets

The first step in the entire process is making sure that the company understands the SDGs and their associated targets, since absent such an understanding, it is impossible for the company to make good decisions regarding the priorities that should be set for SDG-related activities. Understanding begins with a review of all of the SDGs and their targets and consideration of how the issues raised by the SDGs and targets *might* relate to the company's business (including not only internal operations but also its value chain). The goal at this point is to identify targets to which the company could make a critical difference by tackling risks in its own operations and value chain (e.g., extractive companies and companies with large distribution networks can implement measures to reduce road accidents during their operations, thus contributing to one of the targets associated with SDG 3 on good health and well-being). In addition, the company should identify ideas for applying its skills and capability in new ways to advance SDGs (e.g., banks and technology companies might invest in development of new products and services to increase the access of small-scale industrial and other enterprises to financial services, which is one of the targets associated with SDG 9 on industry, innovation, and

---

[5] Integrating the SDGs into Corporate Reporting: A Practical Guide (Global Reporting Initiative, Principles for Responsible Investment and United Nations Global Compact, 2018), 5.

infrastructure). A thorough review of the SDGs also makes it easier for companies to understand how actions can actually contribute to more than one SDG or target at a time (e.g., a renewal energy project advances access to basic services (SDG target 1.4) and access to affordable, reliable and modern energy services (SDG target 7.1).[6]

Principled Prioritization

The next step, which is central to the entire reporting process, is conducted what the drafters of the SDG Reporting Guide described as "principled prioritization" of the SDG targets in order to identify those targets that the company will focus on during its efforts to make a contribution to the SDGs. It was explained that this approach was intended to align with the United Nations Guiding Principles on Business and Human Rights, the Ten Principles of the United Nations Global Compact, the OECD Guidelines for Multinational Enterprises, and the related OECD Due Diligence Guidance for Responsible Business Conduct. As subsequently explained inmore detail0, principled prioritization should be conducted through two entry points: risks to people and the environment (entry point A), which focuses on identifying the most severe negative impacts on people and the environment that are linked to the company's operations and value chain and the SDG targets to which they relate, thus identifying opportunities to tackle these risks in ways that maximize positive outcomes for people and the environment and therefore for the SDGs; and beneficial SDG-related products, services, and investments (entry point B), which focuses on how the company can make additional contributions to achievement of the SDGs by applying its knowledge, skills, and other capabilities to develop products, services, or investments that benefit people and the environment and deliver them in ways that minimize any negative impacts.[7]

The purposes and benefits of engaging in principled prioritization were described as follows in the SDG Reporting Guide[8]:

---

[6] Id. at 10.

[7] Id. at 7 and 11.

[8] Id. at 7.

- Aligning the company's strategy, efforts, and allocation of resources with SDG targets in a way that properly reflects their significant impacts based on an orderly and deliberate assessment of the risks to people and the environment and the company's capabilities with respect to the development and delivery of beneficial products, services, and investments.
- Ensuring that the company's disclosures in its sustainability reporting are a true reflection of the significant impacts that have been prioritized internally and that shape how senior management defines company strategy and allocates resources.
- Identifying and describing new actions necessary in order for the company to contribute to the SDGs as opposed to simply disclosing existing efforts, although such disclosures are obviously important to users of the information. Principled prioritization is not only a tool for reporting on the current state of affairs, but should be used as a driver of realignment of the company's strategies to specific SDG targets and the opportunities associated with pursuing and achieving those targets.
- Avoiding "cherry-picking," which means selecting goals and targets based on what is easiest for companies rather than what accounts for the highest priorities; and "'SDG-washing," which means simply reporting on positive contributions to the SDGs and ignoring important negative impacts that also need to be addressed.

When undertaking the principled prioritization process, companies need to avoid thinking that certain SDGs are more important than others. Each of the SDGs and their associated targets are necessary elements of the universal goal of sustainable development and the goal for any specific company is to identify the entry points where it can have the most significant impact on certain SDGs given its business model, resources, skills, and capabilities. Using two entry points for the process also opens up more possibilities for companies to contribute. In some cases, the best approach is to focus on addressing and mitigating the risks of negative actual and potential impacts; however, companies should not confine their lenses on the SDGs to risk management but instead should search for ways to contribute through new products, services, and investments that can improve the company's financial performance and make it a more sustainable enterprise.

Stakeholder Engagement

Implicit in the process of principled prioritization of SDG goals and targets is identifying those issues and topics that are the most material to the company and thus warrant attention in the company's sustainability reporting. In order to identify the topics that should be highlighted in the reports, consideration needs to be given to the needs and expectations of the users of those reports: the company's stakeholders. The SDG Reporting Guide noted that engagement with affected stakeholders (or, where this is not possible, proxy stakeholders who have knowledge of stakeholder interests and perspective), expert stakeholders, and internal stakeholders is essential for companies to identify the material topics to be covered in their reports.[9] While stakeholders can be positively and negative affected by a company's operations or value chain, it is particularly important that companies engage with stakeholders that are likely to be negatively affected (e.g., employees, contract workers, supply chain workers, consumers, community members, etc.), either directly or through their representatives (e.g., trade unions or community leaders). Particular attention should be paid to engaging with vulnerable groups such as migrant workers, women, young people, persons with disabilities, and indigenous peoples. Expert stakeholder engagement can be used as a means for gathering information and opinions from persons who have insights and understanding on the business or its industry and one or more particular aspects of sustainability (e.g., water, human rights, anti-corruption). Potential expert stakeholders include national or international nongovernmental organizations (NGOs), national or international trade union federations, academics, representatives of other companies, consultants, lawyers, and investors with sustainability expertise.

---

[9] Integrating the SDGs into Corporate Reporting: A Practical Guide (Global Reporting Initiative, Principles for Responsible Investment and United Nations Global Compact, 2018), 11.

Companies should not neglect the importance of internal stake-holder engagement, which involves discussions among various depart-ments and levels of operations inside the company to ensure the collaboration necessary for effective reporting. In many cases, compa-nies use these discussions to develop new organizational structures and process, such as a cross-departmental task force composed of knowl-edgeable staff or managers from relevant areas of company operations that is tasked with ensuring the information relevant to a particu-lar SDG target prioritized by the company is shared and integrated effectively into all relevant areas of the company's strategy and opera-tions.[10] Internal engagement is also an excellent opportunity to educate employees about the SDGs and their related targets and provide them with training on how their roles in the company's SDG-related strate-gies and goals can be effectively executed. Most employees have little understanding of the SDGs, why they were developed and how they are being pursued by governments, NGO, businesses, civil society, and others. Education makes it easier for employees to contribute to the identification of the company's material SDG-related topics and par-ticipation of this type builds a sense of ownership among employees and improves morale and commitment.

Priority Risks to People and the Environment

Exploration of the first entry point—assessing how priority risks to peo-ple and the environment relate to SDG targets—begins by identifying a full picture of the risks to people and the environment that are linked to the company's operations and value chain. The goal at this point is to identify both actual and potential negative impacts to employees, work-ers, and the environment, based not only on past practices and events but also on what might occur in the future based on what the company does; where it operates, sources or sells; and its value chain.[11] The likelihood of

---

[10] Id.

[11] Id. at 12.

an impact and/or the difficulty in adequately addressing an impact should not be a basis for not including an impact on the list at this point. The goal is to create a comprehensive inventory based on engagement with internal and external stakeholders that expands the company's knowledge base about its SDG-related risks.

Using the entire value chain as the lens is important because the company needs to consider impacts on people outside of its direct employment relationship, such as workers who are contracted by third parties carrying out services in the company's facilities (e.g., security, cleaning, and catering), as well as impacts on people and the environment throughout its upstream (i.e., manufacturing, procurement, and packaging) and downstream (i.e., distribution, sales, customer usage, recycling) supply chain.[12] The SDG Reporting Guide provided an example of how an apparel company might identify and develop ideas to minimize negative impact or increase positive impact and then align them with different SDGs across a value chain that ran across raw materials, suppliers, inbound logistics, company operations, distribution, product use, and product end life[13]:

- With respect to raw materials, a company prioritizes reduction of its negative impact on SDG 15 (Life on Land) by reducing soil degradation
- With respect to its internal operations, a company priorities reduction of its negative impact on SDG 3 (Good Health and Wellbeing) by ensuring safe working environments at its facilities
- With respect to its suppliers, a company prioritizes reduction of its negative impact on SDG 6 (Clean Water and Sanitation) in the supply chain by reducing waste water
- With respect to product end life, a company prioritizes reduction of its negative impact on SDG 12 (Responsible Consumption and Production) through offering increased opportunities for consumers to recycle used apparel

---

[12] Id. at 13.
[13] Id. at 14.

- With respect to its internal operations, a company prioritizes reduction of its negative impact on SDG 8 (Decent Work and Economic Growth) by providing a living wage to all of its employees

Once the initial inventory is completed, the company then turns to the identification of priority risks by considering both the severity of the potential negative impacts on people and the environment and likelihood or probability of occurrence for each of the potential impacts.[14] According to the SDG Reporting Guide, severity included three, potentially overlapping, factors: how grave an impact is or could be; how widespread an impact is or could be; and how hard it is or would be to put right (or remedy) an impact. While the impacts that are most severe and have a high likelihood of occurring should obviously be given the highest priority, attention should also be given to other impacts with the highest potential severity even if their likelihood of occurrence is relatively low. For example, the science relating to nuclear power has evolved to the point where the likelihood of a major accident has been substantially reduced; however, given that the negative impact of a nuclear accident are so severe it must be placed high on any prioritized list. Special attention should be paid to identifying and prioritizing "salient" human right issues, which by their nature can be difficult for any one company to address effectively on its own yet are nonetheless significant societal risks as to which all companies have a responsibility (i.e., according to the United Nations Guiding Principles on Business and Human Rights, all companies, regardless of their size and sector, to respect human rights across their operations and value chains).[15]

---

[14] Id. at 13.

[15] For further discussion of "salient" human rights, see https://ungpreporting.org/resources/salient-human-rights-issues/ A company's salient human rights issues are those human rights that stand out because they are at risk of the *most severe negative impact* through the company's activities or business relationships, and the concept of salience in this context uses the lens of *risk to people*, not the business, as the starting point, while recognizing that where risks to people's human rights are greatest, there is strong convergence with risk to the business. The severity of salience is based on how grave and how widespread the impact would be and how hard it would be to put right the resulting harm. Id.

The drafters of the SDG Reporting Guide, which included the GRI, made it clear that they believed that the steps laid out in the guide were consistent with the GRI Standards and facilitated the efforts of companies to report based on the GRI Reporting Principles as opposed to creating more work. In particular, they argued that the steps in the guide were aligned with the "materiality assessment" in the GRI Reporting Principles that required companies to conduct sufficient due diligence to ensure that their reports covered topics that reflected their *significant* economic, environmental, or social impacts, or that substantively influence the assessments and decisions of stakeholders.[16] Assuming that the process of principled prioritization is carried out in a comprehensive manner with extensive stakeholder engagement, it also satisfied the requirements in the GRI Reporting Principles related to Stakeholder Inclusiveness, Sustainability Context, Materiality, and Completeness.

Once the priority risks to people and the environment linked to the company's operations and value chain have been identified, the company should link them back to the SDGs and their targets using the thorough understanding of the goals and targets gained earlier in the entire process. The end product of this process obviously depends on the prioritized risks and the company's specific business model and the leverage that it provides the company with respect to addressing a particular SDG or target; however, the examples provided in the SDG Reporting Guide are illustrative[17]:

- A priority risk of discrimination against women in the company's workplace relates to SDG target 5.1: "end all forms of discrimination against women and girls everywhere";
- An actual or potential limitation on freedom of association impairs workers' labor rights in general and is relevant to SDG target 8.5: "achieve full and productive employment and decent

---

[16] Integrating the SDGs into Corporate Reporting: A Practical Guide (Global Reporting Initiative, Principles for Responsible Investment and United Nations Global Compact, 2018), 12.

[17] Id. at 13–14.

work for all women and men, including for young people and persons with disabilities, and equal pay for work of equal value";

- Risks related to climate change are linked to targets under SDG 13 on climate action and can also be linked to SDG 2 on hunger eradication (through sustainable agriculture), SDG 3 on good health and well-being, and SDG 7 on affordable and clean energy;
- Low wages for workers in a company's supply chain relate directly to SDG 1 on ending poverty and target 1.2 to reduce poverty at least by half, as well as to SDG 10 on reducing inequalities and target 10.1 to sustain income growth of the bottom 40 percent at a rate higher than the national average.[18]

Business Opportunities Ffrom Contributing to the SDGs

The second entry point of principled prioritization calls on companies to move away from traditional risk management thinking to focus on opportunities afforded by the drive toward contribution to the SDGs and their targets to develop beneficial products, services, or investments that will have actual and potential positive impacts or benefits.[19] Companies may already have products, services, or investments that benefit certain SDG targets and, if so, the opportunity to scale these existing benefits should be considered at this point. In addition, however, this is the point where opportunities to apply the company's skills and capabilities to create new products, services, or investments that address the same SDG targets as well as additional ones that have not been on the company's agenda in the past should be considered provided they can also create new value for the company.

Ideas regarding opportunities can be gathered from various resources such as the "Better Business Better World" report available through the

---

[18] The SDG Reporting Guide encouraged companies to think beyond the obvious regarding the range of SDGs and targets that might be addressed by a particular action. For example, in addition to the SDGs and targets relating to low wages in the supply chain mentioned in the text, an argument can be made that requiring supply chain partners to provide living wages to their workers creates benefits for good health and wellbeing (SDG 3) and quality education (SDG 4). Id. at 14.

[19] Id. at 14.

Business and Sustainable Development Commission (http://report.businesscommission.org/), which identifies the 60 biggest market opportunities related to the achievement of the SDGs in the areas of food and agriculture (e.g., reducing food waste in the value chain, product reformulation, technology in large-scale farms, microirrigation, and urban agriculture); cities (e.g., affordable housing, road safety equipment, water and sanitation infrastructure, office sharing and car sharing); energy and materials (e.g., expansion of renewables, resource recovery, energy access, shared infrastructure, energy efficiency, and carbon capture and storage); and health and well-being (e.g., weight management programs, better disease management, better maternal and child health, and health care training).[20] The categories are broad enough that any company, regardless of its size and type of operations, can find at least one opportunity that is related to its core competencies and is reasonably attainable. In many cases, companies find that there are multiple opportunities that can be pursued simultaneously while retaining a tight focus. For example, opportunities and goals related to health and well-being, such as weight and disease management and child health can be paired with participation in projects related to food and agriculture, such as dietary switch, reducing food waste, and sustainable and urban agriculture.

The SDG Reporting Guide provided several examples of ideas and strategies that might emerge from consideration of the second entry point.[21] For example, companies might tailor existing products and services to meet the unique and specific needs of particular groups of people who are marginalized and discriminated against or who face particular barriers to accessing education, jobs, basic services or other benefits, thereby taking action to address SDG 10 on reducing inequalities. Another approach relies on developing new products and services to support a sustainability cause, such as a financial services company that creates innovative financial tools to provide needed capital to emerging businesses working on bringing environmentally friendly or socially beneficial products and services to new markets. Partnerships are another way

---

[20] Executive Summary: Better Business Better World (Business & Sustainable Development Commission, January 2017), 8–10.

[21] Id. at 15.

to make a contribution, such as a company that collaborates with local indigenous peoples to create new programs for sustainable management of forests in line with SDG 15 on life on land. A company might also utilize its skills and competencies to address an SDG that is somewhat far afield from its core business, such as a communications company that uses its technology to enable children in remote communities to access education, thus contributing to multiple SDGs and targets including SDG 4 (education), SDG target 8.7 (eradication of child labor), and SDG 1 (reduction of poverty).

Once the initial brainstorming for ideas regarding beneficial products, services, and investment is completed, attention needs to turn to prioritization based on the significance of the benefits to society and the significance of the benefits to the company's own business. Measurements of the significance of positive sustainability impacts are challenging and should take into account not only financial measures (e.g., the reduced cost of drinking water for poor populations or the lowered cost of bringing clean energy to consumers), but also environmental and social metrics (e.g., the number of poor people who benefit from a product or service or the number of households reached with a recycling program). While positive measures are important, companies should not ignore the costs associated with a particular product, service or investment, including "opportunity costs" and any expenses related to mitigating any risks to people or the environment that might be created by the project.[22]

Selecting Priority SDG Targets

At this point in the process of principled prioritization, the company should have a robust collection of two sets or priority SDG targets from each of the entry points that is based on an assessment of risks to people and the environment and an exploration of beneficial products, services, or investments. While each of the targets is important, many companies will not be able to address all of them simultaneously and will need

---

[22] Id.

to make difficult decisions among them based on available resources. In some cases, there will be overlap between the two lists, which makes the particular target particularly attractive because it allows the company to address both risk and opportunities. For example, the SDG Reporting Guide suggested that a technology company that has developed a hotline service for workers suffering abuse might bring it to the attention of companies whose supply chain it was a part of, thus furthering a business opportunity, while also requiring that companies in its own supply chain use the service, thus addressing the risk of poor working conditions among its suppliers.[23] Final decisions should not be made without additional consultations with stakeholders to ensure that their needs and expectations are fully understood and addressed. Expert stakeholders are also an important resource and can assist the company with understanding and deploying sophisticated tools such as the materiality mapping process developed by the Sustainability Accounting Standards Board (https://materiality.sasb.org/) to identify the sustainability issues that are most likely to affect the financial condition or operating performance of companies.

The SDG Reporting Guide emphasized that companies need to take into account the risks to their business when deciding which SDGs and associated targets are most relevant and material to them and their stakeholders. While sustainability is important in its own right, companies must still be prepared to make the business case for allocating resources toward SDG targets. The best way to do this is to be able to demonstrate that each priority SDG target is related to a specific type of business risk such as reputational risks; financial, legal or regulatory risks; risks to business continuity; risks related to the recruitment, retention, and productivity of employees; or the risk of lack of innovation. The SDG Reporting Guide noted that companies can reduce many of these business risks by taking on the risks to people and the environment highlighted by the SDGs and thus protecting and creating value for the company by making it an employer, partner, supplier, customer, brand, or investment of choice.[24]

---

[23] Id.
[24] Id. at 17.

The output of priority SDG targets from the principled prioritization process becomes an important input into determination of the topics that a company will be covering in its sustainability reporting. The GRI Reporting Framework calls on companies to follow the "materiality principle" in determining the boundaries of their reports and companies should keep this in mind when selecting their SDG targets. Specifically, the targets should reflect the company's significant economic, environmental, and social impacts, both negatively and positively, and substantively influence the assessment and decision of stakeholders. However, even though multiple targets may be material, not all of them are of equal importance, thus prioritization is necessary in order to provide report users with a properly weighted picture of company's sustainability priorities and strategies. As mentioned earlier, stakeholder engagement is essential to ensure that the company understands what stakeholders take into account when assessing the company and making decisions on whether to seek employment with the company, purchase and use the company's products or provide the company with financial support.

Defining Business Goals and Objectives

Once the SDG targets have been prioritized, the company needs to define the specific business goals and objectives for each of its targets. The SDG Reporting Guide recommended that when addressing the priority SDG targets based on risks to people and the environment, companies should identify strategies and specific objectives that go beyond just avoiding harm to include finding and executing on opportunity to maximize positive outcomes in order to support systematic and durable change. For example, a company should not simply adopt and publish policies prohibiting harassment and discrimination of workers in the operations of its supply chain partners, but should also work with local organizations to provide training to managers of its suppliers to identify inappropriate behaviors and work directly with the suppliers to ensure that they provide workers with access to complaints mechanisms and supporting resources. At the same time, the company can support educational programs for women working for suppliers on how to respond to harassment and discrimination and those programs can be expanded to include women's health issues.[25]

When setting objectives for new or adapted products, services, or investments to contribute to one or more of the SDGs, consideration needs to be given to both positive and negative impacts. For example, a company may be interested in investing in the delivery of electricity to poor populations; however, the benefits of such a program will be limited if the processes associated with producing and delivering the electricity have a high environmental footprint. Another illustration of the dilemma that companies might face in balancing positive and negative impacts is when the idea is to build a new renewable energy facility to reduce dependence on fossil fuels and provide energy to underserved communities but the cost is displacement of local indigenous communities without their consent.[26]

The SDG Reporting Guiding recommended that companies take into account planetary boundaries and other thresholds established based on social and natural science when setting their own corporate objectives with respect to SDG targets. For example, the Science Based Targets Initiative is a collaborative undertaking of the CDP, the UN Global Compact, World Resources Institute, and the World Wide Fund for Nature to assist companies in setting, announcing, and meeting science-based emissions reduction targets. Companies should also consult extensively with their stakeholders regarding objectives to understand their expectations and establish a framework for explaining to stakeholders how and why the specific objectives were established.[27] Another resource is the inventory of business tools compiled by the SDG Compass that inventories commonly used business tools that may be useful when assessing a company's impact on the SDGs.[28]

For each of the objectives the company must also select an appropriate set of qualitative and quantitative indicators that can be used to measure progress and report the impacts of the company's efforts to contribute

---

[25] Id. at 19.

[26] Id.

[27] Id.

[28] See Inventory of Business Tools—SDG Compass (https://sdgcompass.org/business-tools/)

toward the SDG targets.[29] Quantitative measures—numerical metrics, ratios, and percentages—should be established based on applicable disclosure standards and guidelines and standard sectorial practices (e.g., competitors and other comparable companies). Quantitative measures are more challenging to develop; however, they are an important and necessary part of the story because they provide users of the report with context presented in the form of a narrative discussion that explains how and why a company identifies, analyzes, and responds to its actual and potential impacts. The SDG Reporting Guide illustrated the mix of the two types of measures by collecting indicators relating to water purification at different levels of a company's operations. Potential quantitative measures included money spent on manufacturing and research and development; water purification table sales revenues; number of water purification tablets sold and consumer information provided with the tablets; purified water consumed in percentage; and reduction in the incidence of waterborne diseases in percentage. At the same time, companies can describe what resources could positively or negatively affect the SDG targets, what activities are undertaken and what is generated through those activities and what changes occurred in the target population and how are those changes related to the company's activities.[30]

The best sustainability reporting seamlessly combines qualitative information regarding outputs of a particular project or activity and quantitative descriptions of the impacts, hopefully positive, associated with those outputs. For example, when a company decides to address SDG targets relating to health it may do so by supporting local programs to educate

---

[29] An extremely useful resource for companies is the Inventory of Business Tools—SDG Compass (https://sdgcompass.org/business-indicators/), which maps existing business indicators against the SDGs and allows companies to explore commonly used indicators and other relevant indicators that may be useful when measuring and reporting their own contribution to the SDGs. See also the list of international reporting frameworks and indicators in the appendices to Integrating the SDGs into Corporate Reporting: A Practical Guide (Global Reporting Initiative, Principles for Responsible Investment and United Nations Global Compact, 2018),

[30] Integrating the SDGs into Corporate Reporting: A Practical Guide (Global Reporting Initiative, Principles for Responsible Investment and United Nations Global Compact, 2018), 20.

younger children about healthy eating and changing their dietary habits. In this case, one of the qualitative measures of the outputs of the program might be the number of students participating in the project; however, a fuller picture of the company's contribution will come from measuring and discussion various types of impact such as the proportion of students reporting a better understanding or improved knowledge about healthy eating; the proportion of children who report, or for whom it is reported, a reduction in consumption of "unhealthy" foods; and the proportion of children who report, or are assessed to be in, better health.[31]

Identifying and Collecting Quantitative and Qualitative Data

Once the indicators have been selected for measuring and reporting performance against the company's SDG targets, the company needs to identify and collect quantitative and qualitative data for each of the indicators on a regular basis. Relevant data may already be available within the company and stakeholder engagement, particularly with employees and other internal stakeholders, is a useful strategy for designing and executing the data collection process. If data is not readily available for an indicator, the company will either need to develop a process for collecting the data or select a new indicator. The SDG Reporting Guide recommended that indicators should be specific, measurable, achievable, relevant, and time-bound and that companies should assign a single owner to each indicator and ensure there are management processes in place to track each indicator and ensure that steps are being taken to achieve the goals and objectives that the indicator represents. Companies should collect and present data on both an aggregate and regional basis, with regional reporting

---

[31] From Inputs to Impact: Measuring Corporate Community Contributions through the LBG Framework—A Guidance Manual (London: Corporate Citizenship, 2014), 33 (Appendix 4, which includes examples of how to use the depth of impact scale suggested for reporting on corporate community contributions to sustainability goals and targets). See also Appendix 5 of the same publication for lists of typical indicators that can be reported under various types of impact categories including positive changes in people's attitude or behavior, skills and personal development and direct impacts on people's quality of life.

being used to demonstrate impacts on specific populations (e.g., women, elderly people, ethnic groups, people with disabilities, etc.) and/or within particular environmental contexts. Companies should carefully consider the amount and types of resources that will be needed in order to collect the applicable data before a particular indicator is selected.[32]

Report Content and Assessment

With prioritized SDG targets in place and procedures established for collecting the necessary data to track the indicators of performance for each of the targets, the final steps are putting together the content for the company's sustainability reporting and assessing all of the information associated with the reporting process to identify and implement appropriate changes within the organization. The SDG Reporting Guide argued that companies need to include SDG-related information in their reporting cycles to demonstrate how the SDGs are integrated into the company's business strategy, priorities, and objectives and recommended that SDG reporting should be based on established international frameworks whenever possible, taking into account any specific requirements and expectations among the company's internal and external stakeholders. Companies operating on a global scale will need to take into account different regional interests when reporting as well as providing information on universal issues. For example, such companies should report on climate change, an issue that has global impact, but should also ensure that their reporting addresses material topics in key local markets that are often concerned with specific community development and/or local resource management challenges.

The SDG Reporting Guide recommended that companies understand and apply the "4Cs" of effective reporting[33]:

---

[32] Integrating the SDGs into Corporate Reporting: A Practical Guide (Global Reporting Initiative, Principles for Responsible Investment and United Nations Global Compact, 2018), 21.

[33] Id. at 23.

- *Concise:* Concise reporting focuses on the priorities and most material information, and avoids clutter and information overload.
- *Consistent:* Consistent reporting allows for an assessment of performance trends over time; it enables managing and understanding the insights delivered by the reported data.
- *Current:* Current reporting presents a useful window that gives insights into the operations, impacts and potential of business opportunities, rather than a rear-view mirror showing what happened in the past.
- *Comparable:* Comparable reporting allows information users to benchmark performance against peers and also enables businesses to track and assess their impacts, and then make decisions that will improve impacts over time.

As for how the SDG targets should be integrated into sustainability reporting, the SDG Reporting Guide provided the following checklist for report content[34]:

- The company's significant impacts, whether based on risks to people or environment or on beneficial products, services, and investments
- How the company's analysis of these impacts has informed the company's identification of its priority SDG targets
- How stakeholder feedback informed the company's conclusions
- The company's strategy, including objectives (goals) and measurement (indicators) for contributing to the priority SDG targets, recognizing that positive contributions can result from both tackling risks and providing beneficial products or services
- A description of relevant company policies, systems, and processes, including the company's engagement with stakeholders
- Instances where the company has caused or contributed to actual negative impacts, and the action(s) that the company has taken

---

[34] Id.

to enable effective remedy to anyone whose human rights were harmed

- Indicators and data that demonstrate how the company is progressing toward its objectives for contributing to its priority SDG targets and any setbacks it has encountered
- The company's future plans for achieving further progress

Other important things to consider in the reporting process include linking the company's sustainability targets to other relevant international agreements or commitments that address a specific SPG target (e.g., agreements and conventions relating to mitigation of climate change); consulting and adapting recognized standards for reporting on specific SDGs and related targets, such as the recommendations on climate-related disclosures promulgated by the Task Force on Climate-Related Financial Disclosures[35]; preparing the disclosures in a manner that allows them to be easily repurposed for other uses, such as satisfying reporting requirements mandated by regulations and securities exchanges, thus ensuring a consistent message; applying both internal controls and external assurance to enhance accuracy, credibility and overall reporting quality and, in some cases, satisfy the requirements and expectations of investors and other stakeholders; and developing other strategies and tools for communicating the company's sustainability strategy and SDG performance apart from the formal written report (e.g., company website, social media channels, podcasts, events, product and service labeling, marketing, and advertising).[36]

While all stakeholders are important consumers of the company's SDG-related reporting, a great deal of attention has been placed on investors' expectations and needs. Research indicates that investors need and expect a clear description of the process that was used by the company to establish the SDG issues deemed to be material, an explanation of the context in which impacts occur and data is reported on, and an overall narrative that links the sustainability issues back to the company's business

---

[35] Id. at 24 (Box 5.9).

[36] Id.

model and future outlook.[37] In addition, the disclosures need to provide investors with insights into how the directors and members of the management team see and understand the relevant of the SDGs to the company's overall strategy and data regarding SDG-related activities, outputs, outcomes, and impacts of the company that are linked to the company's business model and financial performance. From a governance perspective, investors are interested in understanding the policies and procedures that have been implemented for identifying and responding to risk and opportunities, particularly changes that have been made to the company's business model and/or product and service offerings. Specifically, investors want to understand the positive and negative impacts of the company's strategy and activities through discussions of the following[38]:

- The key elements of the company's competitive advantage and how its impacts contribute to or detract from it;
- Sector specificities, including both context in which the business operates and specific disclosures;
- How the company transforms competitive advantage into business results and how the approach to the SDGs contributes to them;
- The SDGs and targets that are likely to present the greatest business risks and opportunities for the company, through identifying significant risks to people and the environment through the company's operations and value chains;
- How SDG-related outputs, outcomes, and impacts are linked to the market factors driving corporate strategy and, where such information is available, how these trends could potentially affect the company's financial outcomes. Understanding the policies behind the outputs and outcomes is particularly important for companies with large manufacturing operations and complex supply chains;
- The existence of and investment in "enabling effects" (e.g., infrastructure as basis for development);

---

[37] In Focus: Addressing Investors Needs in Business Reporting on the SDGs (Global Reporting Initiative, Principles for Responsible Investment and United Nations Global Compact, 2018), 14.
[38] Id.

- The calculation methodologies and explanation of the business structure help the interpretation of quantitative data;
- Companies should identify and publish material SDG contributions, both positive and negative, including salient human rights issues and relevant KPIs as part of their report.

Investors understand that not all of the 17 SDGs will be equally relevant to all companies and they are not interested in boilerplate discussions across all of the areas. Instead, companies are expected to identify those SDGs that are most relevant to their business as measured by their implications for business strategy and financial performance and qualitatively discuss how the company's SDG-related activities, output outcomes, and impacts affect the primary value drivers of the business.[39] Investors also need and expect a clear description of the process that was used by the company to establish the SDG issues deemed to be material, an explanation of the context in which impacts occur and data is reported on, and an overall narrative that links the sustainability issues back to the company's business model and future outlook.[40] Businesses need to develop a clear picture of the data needs of primary investors through engage and dialogue, and provide both qualitative and quantitative information.

During the investor engagement process, a determination should be made regarding the frequency, format, and channels to present SDG-related information to investors and other key stakeholders. The message that is ultimately developed should be consistent and should be apparent in all communications by the company regarding its SDG-related activities and contributions. Consistency comes from taking an integrated approach and setting the tone and content at the very top of the organization, beginning with the board of directors and all members of the executive team. In fact, the board, or at least a dedicated committee created by the board, should be regularly involved in the process of setting SDG-related strategy and SDG reporting.

---

[39] Id.
[40] Id. at 14.

While the content and formatting of a company's SDG-related report-ing will be driven by the the aforementioned factors—the reporting frame-work and standards selected by the company and the topics that emerge from the principled prioritization process—special consideration should also be given the needs of key stakeholders and the data and analysis they require and expect in order to make decisions regarding their relationships with the company. For example, states have obviously been given a key, if not primary, role in the global drive to pursue and achieve the SDGs and companies can support governmental efforts by collecting and reporting the data that is most salient to governments looking to measure their own progress toward the SDGs. Governments understand that participation from the private sector must be part of their national agendas relating to the SDGs and dialogue between governments and companies should occur to ensure that reporting by companies is both relevant and accessible.[41]

Other stakeholders have their own specific needs as it pertains to SDG-related data and reporting. Investors use SDG-related data to assess risks, including risks related to companies, and new business opportu-nities, and are particularly interested in how companies are transform-ing their competitive advantage in relation to the SDGs into business results and on how relevant the SDGs are to overall company strategies. Civil society organizations assess SDG performance and hold companies accountable as well as press for more transparency; however, the relation-ship with civil society need not be hostile if companies are willing and able to engage with these organizations to tap into their expertise and forge partnerships that can work effectively in the communities in which the company is working on its SDG targets. Consumers have shown an increasing appetite for more sustainable products and services and their choices will be influenced by information on a company's SDG-related performance. Information from the SDG-related reporting by compa-nies can also be used by policymakers and academic researchers to test

---

[41] Integrating the SDGs into Corporate Reporting: A Practical Guide (Global Report-ing Initiative, Principles for Responsible Investment and United Nations Global Com-pact, 2018), 25.

the viability of the universal SDG targets to determine whether changes should be proposed and implemented.[42]

SDG-related reporting, and all of the steps that go into developing and implementing an effective reporting process, is not the end in and of itself, the goal should be to measure and continuously improve the company's contributions to the SDG targets and establish itself as a "good corporate citizen" of the world. Part of all this is to conduct regular and continuous assessments to determine whether the company is meeting the goals and objectives that it has previously established in relation to its priority SDG targets. Even the best laid plans will have shortcoming in certain areas and the goal of the assessment should be to identify performance gaps and create strategies for improvement. In many cases, the company will need to make internal changes in order to promote better coordination and establish ownership, authority, and accountability with regard to the SDG targets. The SDG Reporting Guide suggested, for example, that responsibility for the priority SDG targets related to suppliers should be 'owned' by the department responsible for engaging with and managing suppliers. Other suggestions offered by the SDG Reporting Guide included reviewing and assessing the reporting cycle to ensure that internal reporting processes are synchronized with public disclosures, regularly reviewing the consultation schedule with stakeholders to elicit their input into the reporting process; confirming that the SDG-related reporting is being used as a basis for informed decision making and being integrated into the company's strategies; communicating the company's SDG-related goals and strategies internally so that all employees understand the company's mission and their respective roles and providing relevant training so that employees can make better contributions on their own; and proactively participating in "collective action" by looking for strategic opportunities to collaborate with peers and others to leverage resources, advocate business responsibility, establish sectoral objectives and initiatives or spread the implementation costs of the actions required in order to advance the SDGs.[43]

---

[42] Id.
[43] Id. at 26.

CHAPTER 6

Report Formatting and Presentation

While the formatting and presentation of financial reporting has become somewhat standardized due to regulatory requirements, the development and maturation of professional financial accounting standards and long-standing expectations of consumers of such information, there is no particular template in terms of format, length, and details that applies to sustainability reports and one can find a wide array of creative approaches to presenting information related to corporate social responsibility (CSR). The persons responsible for preparing sustainability reports should seek out and review comparable reports prepared by peer companies in order to get a sense of how information might be presented and, not unimportantly, the CSR issues that peers have chosen to focus on and how they are describing and measuring progress on those issues.

While international standards like the GRI Standards provide a useful framework for comprehensive CSR verification and reporting, companies should remember that it is important to tailor the information in their reports to the needs and expectations of their specific primary audiences. It has become more and more common among larger companies to generate large reports with glossy pictures, charts, and graphs and detailed breakdowns of data; however, many interested parties prefer to a short executive summary that highlights the most relevant information and provides links to detailed reports, case studies, and other materials. Information should be presented in a manner that reflects the company's overall organizational culture and provides recipients with a sense of what social responsibility means to the company's leaders and employees on a day-to-day basis. Finally, while reporting is certainly a positive public relations tool and companies will be eager to showcase their CSR successes, credibility demands that reports also include transparent assessments of areas in which the company may have failed to achieved its previously announced objectives and disclosures on the reasons for those failures and the steps the company is taking to improve its performance and the metrics that will be used to evaluate how well the remediation is proceeding.

Common Elements and Disclosures in Sustainability Reports

A review of sustainability reports confirms the impressions of Libit and Freier and other commentators regarding the consistent appearance of the following elements and disclosures in such reports[1]:

An opening letter or executive summary from the company's chief executive officer and/or chief CSR/sustainability executive noting the company's commitment to CSR and sustainability-related issues and its willingness to discuss challenges and promote successes relating thereto

The company's CSR or sustainability policy or mission statement and a statement by the board of directors to the effect that it has considered sustainability issues as part of its formulation of the company's strategy; determined the material sustainability factors (as subsequently discussed); and overseen management, monitoring, and reporting on such factors

A description of the material sustainability factors identified by the company including an explanation of the reasons for, and process of, selection of such factors taking into account the business, strategy, business models, and key stakeholders

A presentation of the company's targets for the upcoming reporting period in relation to each material sustainability factor identified

---

[1] Adapted from B. Libit and T. Freier, The Corporate Social Responsibility Report and Effective Stakeholder Engagement (Chapman and Cutler LLP, 2013), available at https://corpgov.law.harvard.edu/2013/12/28/the-corporate-social-responsibility-report-and-effective-stakeholder-engagement/; and "SGX Sustainability Reporting Guide" in Sustainability Guide for Boards: At a Glance (Singapore Institute of Directors, KPMG and SGX, September 2017).

A description of the company's policies, practices, and performance
in relation to each of the identified material sustainability factors
including quantitative information on each factor for the reporting period and a comparison of performance during the period to
previously disclosed targets

Identification and description of the sustainability reporting framework selected by the company including the reasons for the
selection and demonstration of its applicability to the company's
industry, operations, and business model

Assuming, for purposes of illustration, that the company selected the
GRI sustainability reporting framework, which has been adopted
by a substantial percentage of the S & P 500 companies that
prepare and distribute sustainability reports, a series of sections
incorporating disclosures recommended in the GRI reporting
framework:

Economic Considerations: Disclosing the company's impacts on the
economic conditions of its stakeholders and on economic systems
at local, national and global levels

Environmental Issues: Disclosing the company's impacts on living and
nonliving natural systems (i.e., land, air, water, and ecosystems),
including impacts related to inputs (e.g., energy and water), outputs (e.g., emissions, effluents, and waste) as well as environmental compliance and expenditures

Ethics and Integrity: Disclosing the company's values, principles
and standards, and its internal and external mechanisms for
seeking advice on ethical and lawful behavior and reporting
concerns about unethical or unlawful behavior and matters of
integrity

Social Impact: Disclosing the company's impacts on the social systems within which it operates, including those relating to human
rights, society and product responsibility

Stakeholder Engagement: Disclosing the company's stakeholder
engagement during the reporting period and not limiting it solely
to engagement conducted for purposes of preparing the sustainability report A series of sections that include disclosures on the

issues that the company has determined to be of most importance
to each of its key stakeholders:

Shareholders: Addressing the company's business model and corporate governance, including disclosing the role of the board in risk
management, in sustainability reporting and in evaluating CSR
performance

Employees: Addressing diversity, health and safety, training and men-
toring, employee relations, and wages and benefits

Customers: Addressing customer service and privacy

Suppliers: Addressing labor standards and whether suppliers are
required to implement their own CSR programs

Communities: Addressing corporate philanthropy and charitable
contributions, community investment and partnerships, volun-
teerism, and the environmental impact of operations

Governments and Regulators: Addressing lobbying, public policy,
and the effects of and compliance with environmental
regulations

The sustainability report should also include any specific disclosures
that may be required by regulators and/or listing authorities in the case of
companies with shares listed on securities exchanges.[2] In cases where disclosures on sustainability-related issues are already required in traditional
financial reports, those disclosures may be repeated in the sustainability report to ensure consistency among the disclosures in the company's
various public documents. Sustainability reports should be carefully
reviewed in advance of release to ensure that they do not include material information that should have been previously disclosed in satisfaction

---

[2] For example, even though the major U.S. securities exchanges have yet to adopt
comprehensive sustainability-related disclosure requirements, companies listed
on the main market of the London Stock Exchange are required to publish full
details of their greenhouse gas emissions and under the listing requirements of the
Singapore Exchange companies are required to prepare and publish sustainability
reports that discuss the environmental, social, and governance factors that the
board is required to determine as being material and thus subject to monitoring
and management.

of the company's periodic reporting obligations and/or to comply with the requirements of Regulation FD promulgated by the Securities and Exchange Commission and applicable to reporting companies. Since sustainability is, almost by definition, a long-term initiative the plans and projections for future performance on matters such as energy savings and reduction of adverse environmental impacts of operations should be tempered by disclaimers on "forward looking statements" similar to those already commonly used in financial reporting. Setting boundaries for the report is difficult given the lack of formal requirements; however, the time and resources of the committee members and management is limited and the subject matter of the report should be tightly focused on the issues that have the greatest impact on the company's operations and finances and its relationships with key stakeholders.

Finnish Textile and Fashion (FTF), the central organization for textile, clothing, and fashion companies in Finland, suggested several different approaches that companies could use for reporting on their corporate responsibility results including reporting on the company's website; reporting in PDF format, with the report being made available on the website; printed report equivalent to the PDF report, or including a corporate responsibility section in the company's annual report on financial results and other matters required by law and/or securities exchange regulators.[3] Each format has its own specific advantages. For example, FTF noted that if visitors to the website wish to search for specific details within the report, the information is easier to find in an online report. However, if people want to read through the entire report and also print it, a PDF file is more suitable, and pictures, graphs, and tables are also better presented in a PDF.

As for presenting the information in the corporate responsibility report, FTF suggested that the following sections could be used[4]:

1. Introduction of the report's contents and coverage
2. Foreword from the managing director/CEO/board chairperson

---

[3] *Finnish Textile and Fashion Corporate Responsibility Manual* (Helsinki: Finnish Textile & Fashion, 2016), 56.
[4] Id. at 57.

3. Brief summary of the company
4. Overview and description of company's corporate responsibility management
    4.1. Values, strategy, management model
    4.2. Stakeholders (description, engagement, expectations, actions, and indicators)
    4.3. Risks and opportunities
    4.4. Management principles that steer corporate responsibility
        • Principles of responsible business
        • Environmental policy
        • Human resources principles
    4.5. Corporate responsibility organization
5. Corporate responsibility results
    5.1. Evaluation of the relevance of indicators
    5.2. Summary of key results
    5.3. Financial responsibility
    5.4. Environmental responsibility
    5.5. Personnel responsibility
    5.6. Collaboration with partners
    5.7. Product responsibility
6. Corporate responsibility program targets for next two/three years

While each of the afore-listed sections is important, particular attention needs to be paid to presentation of results in each of the five key areas of corporate responsibility (i.e., §§ 5.3–5.7), FTF recommended that companies begin by briefly setting out how each area is managed and then continue with an explanation of the importance of each topic to the company, as well as the targets, actions, and results presented in terms of quantifiable indicators that include both good and bad outcomes. Companies should provide an explanation as to why targets have been achieved or missed and should also provide an assessment of how the company has performed vis-à-vis comparable companies and their industry as a whole provided that reliable comparative data is available. Since corporate responsibility is a continuous process, rather than a state that is attained and remains static, the report should put the company's status in perspective and results from previous years should be included in summary fashion in order to assist readers in understanding trends in each of the areas. In the same vein, the last section should be used as an opportunity to present targets for future years, perhaps three years out, so that the company and readers of the report can monitor progress. Other important subjects that are emphasized in many of the widely used reporting frameworks include stakeholder engagement and discussion of the managerial processes used to identify and quantify the reporting topics that are most material to the company's business and meeting the expectations of stakeholders. If the company bases its reporting on a particular reporting framework, such as the GRI, the requirements of the framework should be described along with a summary of the steps that were taken by the company in order to comply with those requirements.[5]

Stakeholder Engagement and Development of Material Disclosure Issues

Regardless of which reporting framework is used or the decisions made regarding the formatting and ordering of the presentation of information, companies must take into account its activities, impacts, and the substantive expectations and interests of its stakeholders. In a publication focusing on how small businesses can utilize the GRI standards, the GRI and the International Organization of Employers recommended that sustainability reports should identify the company's stakeholders and explain how the company has responded to their reasonable expectations and interests.[6] This should be done by describing and mapping the stakeholders to whom the company considers itself accountable and discussing the process and outcomes of the company's stakeholder engagement processes. The sustainability report should identify and describe the key interests of the various stakeholder groups and show how the company

---

[5] Id. at 58.

[6] Small Business Big Impact: SME Sustainability Reporting from Vision to Action (Amsterdam and Geneva: Stichting Global Reporting Initiative and the International Organization of Employers, 2016), 8–10. The publication is available for download at www.globalreporting.org.

has responded to stakeholder concerns, policies, and relevant standards. The following list illustrates engagement mechanisms and examples of key interests for various stakeholder groups:

- *Customers* may be engaged through meetings and customer visits/ audit and their key interests may include quality of products, reliability of supply, and product pricing.
- *Employees* may be engaged through periodic performance reviews, management committees, surveys, Intranet/newsletters, site meeting, and community and wellness meetings and their interests may include workplace health and safety and career development.
- *Governmental officials and regulators* may be engaged through meetings, reports, site visits, and submissions and their key interests may include safety of products and compliance.
- *Shareholders and investment community* members may be engaged through periodic reports filed in compliance with regulatory requirements (including financial results performance), annual shareholders' meetings, corporate website and investor briefings, and forums and their key interests may include financial performance, governance and innovation.
- *Local communities* may be engaged through industry bodies, educational institutions, charities, and staff engagement in local events and their key interests may include community impacts, education, product access, infrastructure, and support for services.
- *Suppliers* may be engaged through site visits/audits and meetings and their key interests may include business ethics, compliance, and quality/reliability.

Emerging standards, including the GRI, also attempt to ensure that companies remain focused in their sustainability reporting by emphasizing "materiality," which means that reporting should be confined to coverage of topics that reflect the company's significant economic, environmental, and social impacts or substantively influence the assessments and decisions of its stakeholders. The authors of the GRI publication urged companies to take into account current topics and issues that represent significant risks for the company and its areas of operation; the main sustainability interests, topics, and indicators raised by stakeholders; the main topics and future challenges for the company's sector or region as reported by peers, competitors, or expert bodies with recognized credentials in the field; and relevant laws, regulations, international agreements, or voluntary agreements with strategic significance to the company and its stakeholders. The engagement process and the identification of key interests of each of the company's stakeholders provide the basis for the disclosure and reporting committee to identify and recommend to the entire board for approval a list of the issues that are most material to the company for strategic development and sustainability reporting. These issues become the centerpiece of the organization of the company's sustainability report. Examples of material issues that might be selected include the following[7]:

- *Employee health and safety:* Ensuring our employees work in a safe environment, which meets or exceeds relevant regulatory expectations, addresses health and safety concerns as they arise and mitigates opportunities for reoccurrence of incidents;
- *Product quality and safety to customers*: Choosing materials from quality sources, complying with current "good manufacturing practice," and delivering fit-for-purpose, safe products to customers that adhere to, or exceed strict regulatory standards in all jurisdictions served by the company;
- *Corruption and bribery*: Business must be conducted with transparency, and free from unethical persuasion in every aspect of the company's business from identifying product sources, through development of new products, transactions with regulatory bodies, and sale to customers;
- *Ethical purchasing and human rights in the supply chain*: Responsibility to partners to ensure our product line is free from human rights concerns such as forced labor and trafficking, unsafe labor standards, and unfair treatment;

---

[7] Based on Mayne Pharma Group Limited Sustainability Report 2016, 12, https://maynepharma.com/media/1896/myx_2016_sustainability_report.pdf

- *Compliance:* Responsibility to drive compliance with legal and regulatory requirements applicable to our global business including training programs, continuous improvement, and striving for best practice;
- *Resource use and waste management:* Includes energy usage during manufacture and logistics, water usage, and waste as a by-product of manufacture.

Integrating Financial and Nonfinancial Reporting

While CSR reporting has already evolved significantly, there will no doubt be important and interesting changes in the future as the appetite of the various stakeholder groups, particularly investors, for information on CSR management and corporate governance generally grows.[8] There is already intense discussion about nonfinancial reporting, sometimes referred to as "extra-financial reporting" or "intangibles" reporting, that would cover operational activities that are not yet formally regulated but are already embedded in global social responsibility standards and best practices regarding ethical business conduct. In fact, a number of companies already include both financial and nonfinancial information in their reports to the investors and other stakeholders and it is expected that disclosure requirements in investor reports will continue to be changed to incorporate more analysis of the impact of environmental and social responsibility initiatives on economic performance and the overall well-being of the communities that are served by the company.

A popular format for integrating financial and nonfinancial reporting is the "triple bottom line," which facilitates incorporation of economic, environmental, and social considerations into performance measurement and disclosures; however, others have argued that additional dimensions

---

[8] The discussion in this section is adapted from P. Hohnen (Author) and J. Potts (Editor). 2007. *Corporate Social Responsibility: An Implementation Guide for Business.* Winnipeg, Canada: International Institute for Sustainable Development, 2007, 70.

should be included such as culture and ethics.[9] Jackson et al. explained that TBL reporting connects traditional financial reporting with the business's everyday activities in a way that provides a broader awareness of the impact of the business on society and argued that TBL report-ing was important because it expanded stakeholders" knowledge of the company to include not only financial performance but also the positive and negative impacts that the company and its operations are having on the environment and society.[10] TBL reporting involves a commitment by the company to provide its stakeholders with additional information and to communicate that information in ways that the stakeholders can understand and which are consistent with their expectations. Stakehold-ers are demanding transparency and TBL reporting must be balanced and include negative items accompanied by an explanation by the company as to what it is doing to correct unsustainable results and impacts. By increasing knowledge about the sustainability-related impacts of the com-pany's operations, TBL reporting builds relationships among stakeholders and enables stakeholders to participate in the improvement processes that are necessary for the company to pursue and achieve sustainability.

Jackson et al. pointed out that several arguments had been made against TBL reporting, beginning with the concern that focused and detailed sustainability reporting might expose significant shortcom-ings in the ways that companies actually operate in relation to the flow-ery commitments they might have made in their public statements.[1] Of course, companies should not expect to be able to "get away" with announcing sustainability goals and commitments and not being held to account by stakeholders. In fact, sustainability commitments should not be made without performance metrics and plans and procedures for collecting and reporting on the data that stakeholders would reason-

---

[9] For further discussion of the "triple bottom line" and other dimensions of sustainability, see Gutterman, A. 2019. *Responsible Business: A Guide to Corporate Social Responsibility for Sustainable Entrepreneurs* Oakland, CA: Sustainable Entrepreneurship Project, 2019 available at www.seproject.org.

[10] Jackson, A., K. Boswell, and D. Davis. November, 2011. "Sustainability and Triple Bottom Line Reporting—What is it all about?" *International Journal of Business, Humanities and Technology*, 1, no. 3, pp. 55–56, 58.

[11] Id. at 56.

ably need in order for them to determine the progress of the company with respect to those commitments. A related concern is the possibility that critics may focus on ethical problems that come to light as a result of reporting on negative impacts, thus damaging the company's reputation and undermining the positive messaging that the company is trying to send regarding its shift toward becoming more environmentally and socially responsible.[12]

Another concern about the implementation of TBL reporting is that in order for it to be completely effective, the corporate environment has to be eradicated and rebuilt.[13] Jackson et al. noted that companies have structured their policies and operations around the requirements of the financial regulations that have traditionally driven reporting and that adding the TBL to the company's reporting process would require new policies and extensive readjustments of the company's operations that would be costly, time-consuming, and stressful and require that employees receive training to prepare them for new responsibilities and tasks.[14] New responsibilities and tasks for the workforce also means that individual performance evaluation metrics will need to be changed, which will almost certainly cause some disruption and confusion among employees. At the same time, however, surveys have shown that a strong commitment to sustainability has a number of positive impacts on employees including improvements in morale and reductions in turnover. The new policies and procedures associated with TBL reporting are also likely to improve productivity over the long term and provide insights into products and processes that will ultimately improve the quality of the customer's experience with the company.

---

[12] Id. at 58.

[13] Id. at 57.

[14] Id.

CHAPTER 7

CSR Communications

In addition to formal reporting on corporate responsibility, companies should consider how their corporate responsibility activities can be integrated into their overall corporate communications strategies and activities and their marketing activities. Finnish Textile and Fashion (FTF) cautioned that corporate social responsibility (CSR) communications should be appropriate in light of the company's nature, size, operating methods and potential risks related to corporate responsibility, and recommended that companies focus their communications efforts on matters that are essential from the business perspective, are of interest to stakeholders, and include potential operational and reputational risks. For example, since consumers are interested in the origin of the products that are marketing and sold by the company, communications should include transparent information on all stages of the value chain including a description of how the company monitors the environmental and social responsibility of supply chain partners and data on compliance by those partners with company requirements. Information on environmental and social responsibility aspects of the inputs to products should also be presented and corporate communications are a good opportunity for companies to describe the process that is followed in designing and manufacturing products including consideration of methods for managing the environmental footprint of products over their entire lifecycle of use and disposal.[1]

Finnish Textile and Fashion also noted that disclosures regarding a company's corporate responsibility activities extend beyond sustainability reporting and other formal corporate communications to include marketing activities and companies will naturally want to include their corporate

---

[1] *Finnish Textile and Fashion Corporate Responsibility Manual* (Helsinki: Finnish Textile & Fashion, 2016), 58.

responsibility successes in efforts to promote its brand. However, presentation of environmental and social responsibility in advertising and marketing materials are subject to the same fundamental principles as any other information and companies need to ensure the information is not misleading or unjustified.[2] Regulators often issue guidelines that cover advertising practices. One example referred to by FTF was the policies of the Finnish Competition and Consumer Authority relating to consumer rights in connection with environmental marketing, which emphasized that claims made in marketing must be backed up by evidence and that companies should avoid presenting minor environmental impacts that were insignificant in view of the company's overall activities if other, clearly more significant environmental impacts were played down. Finnish Textile and Fashion pointed that companies can use environmental certification and branding in their marketing activities provided they comply with the requirements and instructions of the certifying bodies. Signaling social responsibility in marketing is more difficult. Companies certified as to social responsibility in accordance with the SA8000 standard are listed in a public database; however, there is currently no branding for SA8000. Some companies do attempt to incorporate social responsibility into their marketing activities by identifying the country of origin in their product labeling and/or describing the social responsibility audit and certification procedures used in each of the production phases for the company's products.[3]

ISO 26000 also emphasized the important roles that internal and external communications play in social responsibility including[4]:

---

[2] Id. at 59.

[3] Companies certified as to social responsibility in accordance with the SA8000 standard are listed in a public database; however, there is currently no branding for SA8000. Some companies do attempt to incorporate social responsibility into their marketing activities by identifying the country of origin in their product labeling. Id.

[4] ISO 26000 Guidance on Social Responsibility (Geneva: International Organization for Standardization, 2010), 77.

- Raising awareness both within and outside the organization on its strategies and objectives, plans, performance, and challenges for social responsibility
- Demonstrating respect for social responsibility principles
- Helping to engage and create dialogue with stakeholders
- Addressing legal and other requirements for the disclosure of information related to social responsibility
- Showing how the organization is meeting its commitments on social responsibility and responding to the interests of stakeholders and expectations of society in general
- Providing information about the impacts of the organization's activities, products, and services, including details of how the impacts change over time
- Helping to engage and motivate employees and others to support the organization's activities in social responsibility
- Facilitating comparison with peer organizations, which can stimulate improvements in performance on social responsibility
- Enhancing an organization's reputation for socially responsible action, openness, integrity, and accountability, to strengthen stakeholder trust in the organization

Section 7.5.2 of ISO 26000 described the necessary and appropriate characteristics of information relating to social responsibility as including completeness, understandability, accuracy and verifiability, balance, timeliness, and accessibility and noted that organizations can select from a wide range of methods for communication including meetings, public events, forums, reports, newsletters, magazines, posters, advertising (including public statements to promote some aspect of social responsibility), letters, voicemail, live performance, video, websites, podcasts (website audio broadcast), blogs (website discussion forums), product inserts and labels, media activities (e.g., press releases, interviews, editorials and articles), submissions to government bodies or public inquiries, participation in social responsibility interest groups, and articles in communications instruments aimed at peer organizations.[5]

When developing a communications strategy and program relating to social responsibility, each of the organization's key stakeholders should be considered and plans should be made to tailor communications with stakeholders to the social responsibility issues that are of greatest concern to them. For example, communications with employees should raise general awareness about and support for CSR and related activities; communications with suppliers should explain the organization's CSR-related procurement requirements; and communications with consumers relating products (e.g., product labeling and other product information) should address their expectations regarding how the company integrates safety and sustainability into the design and production of its products.

Since there is so much that any one organization might choose to communicate on with respect to CSR, difficult decisions need to be made about what information and message are disseminated since too much communication can confuse stakeholders as much as it informs and educates them. The UN Global Compact suggests that communications strategies by designed with a reference to materiality of particular issues or events to both stakeholders (as determined through engagement with stakeholders) and the business and overall sustainability of the organization itself. When using this framework, the most attention in communications should be given to those issues that are material to both stakeholders and the business of the organization and in those instances communications should be comprehensive and include a statement of the organization's policies and commitments, an assessment of potential impact and a description of relevant performance indicators and measures. As for issues that are considered to be important to its business by the organization but are which not that important to stakeholders, communications may be limited to impacts. In turn, when stakeholders have identified an issue as important, but the organization does not believe the issue is material to its business, communications may be limited, at least

---

[5] Id. at 77–78.

initially, to a description of the organization's approach and policies with respect to the issue.[6]

While organizations need to be proactive in allocating resources to communications and developing a formal communications strategy, it should not be forgotten that communication is a tool to be used as part of the broader and more important CSR activity and requirement of dialogue and engagement with stakeholders. In other words, effective CSR communications flow both ways and all of the communication methods mentioned earlier should include information on how recipients can provide feedback to the organization.[7] Among other things, organizations should leverage the communications process to gather important information from stakeholders regarding the adequacy and effectiveness of the content, media, and the frequency and scope of communication so that they can be improved as needed; set priorities for the content of future communication; and secure verification of reported information by stakeholders, if this approach to verification is used.[8]

The UN Global Compact endorsed the recommendations regarding communications included in ISO 26000 by calling on organizations to ensure that their communications strategies and content were based on the following characteristics[9]:

- Communications should be understandable to intelligent stakeholders and the organization must be careful to ensure that they are not too technical so as to be only understandable to some.
- Communications should respond to the concerns of stakeholders.
- Communications should be accurate, based on solid evidence and accountability, and should not descend into "PR hype."
- Communications should be balanced and trustworthy and not only highlight what the organization does well but also outline

---

[6] *UN Global Compact: Training of Trainers Course Guidance Manual* (New York: UN Global Compact), 53.

[7] ISO 26000 Guidance on Social Responsibility (Geneva: International Organization for Standardization, 2010), 77–78.

[8] Id. at 79.

[9] *UN Global Compact: Training of Trainers Course Guidance Manual* (New York: UN Global Compact), 51.

areas where the organization has performed less well or has not met targets and objectives.

- Communications should respond to issues and events as swiftly as possible and avoid reliance on outdated accounts of historical events that are not of great use to stakeholders.
- Information should be easily accessible and retrievable.

In addition, the UN Global Compact has emphasized the important of stakeholder communications as a means for documenting the organization's performance on its material CSR issues and providing stakeholders with useful and credible information along with evidence to support the organization's progress toward its CSR commitments and targets. CSR communications should educate stakeholders about the relevant issues and build trust that becomes a foundation for continuing engagement and dialogue.[10]

Branding and Reputation

In many ways, communications regarding CSR are a part of the organization's overall strategy to creating and protecting its "brand," which is the way that the organization distinguishes its products, services, and concepts from those of other organizations. Simply put, an organization's brand is what people first think about when they hear the brand name associated with a product or service and what comes to mind is heavily driven by the organization's messaging in the form of marketing and other communications. However, organizations are not in complete control of their brands, since people will also be influenced by the communications of other stakeholders, such as announcements by NGOs that products being sold by a company were manufactured by suppliers that had failed to respect and protect the human rights of their workers. This type of news can significantly harm an organization's reputation and the tarnish on its brand can linger for years, even after clear and strong steps have been taken to address and eliminate human rights issues in the supply chain.

---

[10] Id. at 56.

Each organization needs to understand how its employees, customers, and other stakeholders arrive at their perceptions of the organization's products and services and identify those actions associated with its business model that are likely to have biggest impact on its reputation with stakeholders. For example, while an airline's reputation for luxury and service is certainly important, by far the biggest concern for potential travelers is the carrier's safety record. As such, every airline needs to pay attention to potential weaknesses in its safety programs, not only because of their legal and moral obligations to protect the lives of their passengers but also because news of safety issues will have a hugely adverse reputational impact even if there is never a situation where the airline is found to be at fault for an accident. Assuming that an airline does have adequate safety procedures in place, it needs to continuously communicate with stakeholders regarding safety and the specific steps it has taken with respect to the issue such as investments in new technology and training for pilots and other personnel.

When the subject matter is "good news," such as a strong safety record for an airline, communicating to stakeholders is a welcome activity. However, communication is just as important, albeit far more challenging, when news is not so good and the organization finds itself engaged in dialogue with stakeholders regarding weaknesses in its environmental or social responsibility. For example, Nike has long been one of the most iconic and widely recognized brands in the world, however, for a number of years the company was maligned by critics armed with evidence that Nike, as well as other big brand names, had relied on outsourcing of production activities to factories in which widespread labor rights abuses were occurring. Nike saw sales of its products erode and endured efforts to tie its brand to slavery and sweat shops. Eventually, Nike responded by investing time and effort in inspecting and auditing the factories of its supply chain partners to identify and eradicating labor rights abuses. As a result of these activities and the communications to stakeholders regarding the problems and how they were being resolved Nike was able to rebuild, and in many ways, strengthen its brand and reputation and thrive in the face of competition from numerous firms peddling cheap knockoffs produced in abhorrent working conditions.[11]

As for branding, the UN Global Compact described the following ways in which CSR can influence the brand-building process[12]:

- Embedding CSR into core values that demonstrate responsibility
- Communicating about brand features that demonstrate commitment to CSR including ethical sourcing, environmental protection, and protection of labor rights
- Appealing to the emotions of customers who want to be associated with (and purchase) products that benefit the people that produce them (e.g., Fair Trade coffee)
- Delivering on the organization's public CSR commitments and promises and strategically communicating performance to stakeholders
- Generating trust
- Developing a mission and vision and ensuring that CSR-related promises are kept

Resolving Conflicts or Disagreements with Stakeholders

Section 7.6.3 of ISO 26000 recommends that organization establish procedures for resolution of conflicts or disagreements that may arise with individual stakeholders or with groups of stakeholders. Conflict resolution mechanisms are commonly included in contracts, such as labor and employment agreements, supply agreements, and agreement relating to the purchase and sale of products and services. However, conflicts often arise outside of a formal contractual relationship and organizations must be prepared to engage in dialogue with the affected stakeholders, share necessary information relating to the dispute, and provide stakeholders with forums where they can air their grievances and provide ideas for resolving problems. It is particularly important for organizations to

---

[11] Id. at 43–44.
[12] Id. at 48.

establish procedures that allow internal stakeholders, such as employees, to register complaints, and/or report apparent violations of law or organizational policies without fear of reprisal and with assurance that their complaint or report will be taken seriously and addressed promptly and fully. ISO 26000 requires that organizations make detailed information on the procedures available for resolving conflicts and disagreements accessible to its stakeholders.[13]

Reputation Management

Reputation is an important intangible element of the value of any company, an asset that needs to be carefully monitored and protected. Events over the last two decades, including period of deep financial crisis and serious questions regarding corporate ethics, have eroded public trust in business and have led to serious questions regarding the operation and fairness of free markets. During that period, activities of businesses, particularly those that are perceived as having a negative environmental and social impact, have been exposed to greater scrutiny by web-based participatory media, nongovernmental organizations, and groups throughout civil society. Expectations on business with respect to environmental and social responsibility have also escalated as governments have retreated in many areas, and companies are now tasked with demonstrating commitment to assisting with sweeping global issues such as climate change, income inequality, poverty, health, and human rights. As a result, corporate missteps, even those that are not intentional and/or arguably well outside of their reasonable scope of influence, are likely to expose companies and their leaders to immediate and stunningly strong criticism from politicians, regulators, consumers, investors, employees, and the public at large, and the fallout will likely include not only short-term financial costs but long-term damage to the company's reputation and brand.[14]

The challenges for companies have been exacerbated by an explosion of the events, including sometimes unforeseeable changes in stakeholder

---

[13] ISO 26000 Guidance on Social Responsibility. Geneva: International Organization for Standardization, 2010, 79–80.

[14] Bonini, S., D. Court and A. Marchi. June 2009. *Rebuilding Corporate Reputations*. McKinsey Quarterly.

attitudes and expectations, which are now increasingly likely to occur and raise reputational issues. For example, banks and other financial services companies have come under what can only be described as permanent scrutiny from consumers, regulators, and the media for their business performance and practices, a situation that has not only damaged the reputations of many well-known and long-standing companies but has also exposed them to a new wave of competition from upstarts pitching socially responsible business models. Pharmaceutical companies are vulnerable to quality issues with their products that can permanently tarnish their brand in markets where customer trust means everything. Other areas of risk to companies due to their day-to-day operations include supply chain management problems, adverse environmental and health impacts of operations and products, worker safety and overall well-being, and protection of personal information.[15]

In this environment, traditional marketing practices and tools, such as public relations campaigns, are no longer adequate and, in fact, surveys indicate that trust in corporate advertising has significantly eroded. Companies required to address actual or potential crises that threaten their reputation often respond ineffectively, leading to criticism that they are more interested in trying to "spin" the situation as opposed to taking the steps necessary to limit reputational damage. Consultants from McKinsey and Company argued that action—not spin—is needed in order to build strong corporate reputations and companies needed to "enhance their listing skills so that they are sufficiently aware of emerging issues; to reinvigorate their understanding of, and relationships with, critical stakeholders; and to go beyond traditional PR by activating a network of supporters who can influence key constituencies."[16] Among other things, companies needed to adopt more sophisticated tools for reputation management, a relatively new concept in world of corporate communications, and reorganize themselves internally to ensure there is a coordinated approach supported by cross-functional teams to gather intelligence and respond quickly to reputational threats.

---

[15] Id. at 4.
[16] Id. at 2.

Adopting an Integrated Response Approach to Reputation Management

Reputation management has been described as referring to the influencing and controlling of the reputation of an individual or group, such as a business organization.[17] The McKinsey consultants noted that effective reputation management requires collection of information about reputational threats across the organization, analysis of that information in sophisticated ways and concerted cross-functional actions to mitigate those threats, and argued that the traditional organizational approach of most companies that relies on small, central corporate affairs departments is not up to the required tasks. For example, a corporate affairs department generally lacks the skills to engage in the two-way dialogues now required by nongovernmental organizations and other stakeholders and is simply too far removed from the activities of business units to identify all of the potential reputational issues, something that is best assigned to the leaders of those business units as part of their broader strategic role with respect to the activities they have been tapped to oversee. The corporate affairs department also lacks the internal leverage over other groups to ensure a multidisciplinary response to reputational threats and relying only on such a department means that the company is not investing in the systems and tools required for internal communications about, and tracking of, risks to the business from reputational problems.[18]

The McKinsey consultants recommended that companies needed to emphasize three priorities in order to prepare for and respond to the wide array of potential reputational threats that they face today. First, they needed to develop processes for assembling enough facts through a deep understanding of their key stakeholders, especially consumers, and their particular concerns and expectations regarding the company and its

---

[17] https://en.wikipedia.org/wiki/Reputation_management
[18] Bonini, S., D. Court and A. Marchi. June 2009. *Rebuilding Corporate Reputations*. McKinsey Quarterly, 3–4.

products and environmental and social responsibility of businesses in general. Second, companies should focus on the actions that matter most to their stakeholders, and do so in a way that prioritizes transparency about the company's priorities and operations. Third, companies must attempt to influence their key stakeholders using techniques that go beyond the traditional approaches of advertising and public relations and emphasize two-way communications to build awareness among stakeholders about the difficult tradeoffs that companies face in balancing economic, environmental, and social priorities.[19]

Understanding Stakeholders and Their Concerns

One of the first steps in effective reputation management is developing a deep understanding of the reputational issues that matter most to the company's stakeholders and the degree to which the company's products, services, operations, supply chains, and other activities impact those issues. This process should begin with documenting, cataloging, and assessing the current sustainability efforts of the company and benchmarking them against competitors and industry standards. In so doing, the company begins to objectively quantify its reputational risks, prioritize those risks, and implement measures for mitigating and reducing those risks. In addition to this type of analysis, companies need to focus on the perceptions and expectations of key stakeholders, since reputation is often built on perceptions as well as data. Sales and growth are influenced by the perceptions and attitudes of stakeholders regarding the company and its sustainability performance and this means that companies need to identify centers of influence among their stakeholder communities. This generally includes not only traditional stakeholders such as consumers, employees, shareholders, and regulators but also nongovernmental organizations and the media.[20]

Stakeholder understanding and communications has become complicated by the expanded array of tools that stakeholders have to collect information and disseminate their opinions and concerns. Another

---

[19] Id. at 4–5.

[20] Id. at 5–6.

issue for companies is that each stakeholder group has its own unique viewpoint on business and the role that the group should be playing in tasking businesses to adhere to their social contracts. Shareholders are obviously interested in how reputational issues will impact long-term growth prospects for their companies and regulators will be reacting to public opinion on the appropriate laws and regulatory policies for businesses and markets. The McKinsey consultants counseled companies to implement methodologies to assist them in understanding the position and concerns of various stakeholders on reputational issues. Among other things, companies need to identify the key issues for each stakeholder group, anticipate the key questions that stakeholders will ask, the actions that the company can take, and the questions that the company can ask. This process for each of the various stakeholder groups can be illustrated as follows[21]:

- *Consumers and Partners:* The key issues for consumers and partners are avoiding purchases from companies that have reputational issues and which are perceived negatively in the market and by the public. Opportunities for both sides to ask questions are somewhat limited and are generally confined to investment conferences. Actions that can be taken by companies include past financials, consensus estimates, trading information, and implied valuation.
- *Media:* Media includes the Internet, newspapers, and television and the key issues that companies faces from this group of stakeholders is a desire by the media to portray big business issues in a negative light and the lack of in-depth reporting required for a balanced view of the issue. Opportunities for both sides to ask questions are somewhat limited and interactions generally occur through telephone discussions between reporters and representatives of the company's investor relations unit. Actions that can be taken by companies include website content, press releases, management press, sell-side analyst calls and reports, and industry reports.

---

[21] Id. at 7.

- *Shareholders, Analysts, and Investors:* The key issues in the investment community are the effect of reputational issues on share prices and related decisions by investors regarding purchases and dispositions of the company's stock. Opportunities for both sides to ask questions can be found in multiple in-depth meetings with executives of the company at all senior leadership levels and follow-up conversations, if necessary, with representatives of the company's investor relations unit. Actions that can be taken by companies include distribution of past operations and unit-level information, distribution, and explanation of management's future strategy and forecasts, industry outlook, and management background as well as distribution of detailed follow-up information.

- *Regulators:* The key issues for regulator are shaping policies and regulations and monitoring the impact of a company's legal and regulatory compliance performance on consumers, the environment, and society. Opportunities for both sides to ask questions include occasional meetings and calls between regulators and representatives of the company's investor relations unit and semiannual or annual meetings between regulators and senior management. Actions that can be taken by companies include quarterly updates on performance and regular reporting on significant changes in outlook.

- *Civil Society:* Civil society includes activist groups, nongovernmental organizations, labor unions, and so on, and their key issues are advocating for companies to adhere to environmental, social, governance, and economic standards. Opportunities for both sides to ask questions include occasional meetings and calls between stakeholder representatives and representatives of the company's investor relations unit and semiannual or annual meetings between stakeholder representatives and senior management. Actions that can be taken by companies include quarterly updates on performance and regular reporting on significant changes in outlook.

While it is useful to refer to the list of stakeholder groups outlined earlier, the reality is that there are different subgroups within each of them and a wide range of attitudes and concerns that must be considered by businesses when developing strategies for stakeholder engagement and communications. The McKinsey consultants provided an illustration of the attitudinal segments among consumers that a company might need to take into account. For example, companies will, hopefully, have positive relationships with consumers who are believers in the system and the company, educated and well-off, and for these customers the strategy of the company should be continuing to build the relationship and encouraging the customers to be positive influencers on behalf of the company. At the same time, companies need to be mindful of consumer segments that are skeptical and/or distrustful about business, uninvolved, or who have to yet form opinions. Even though these segments tend to have relatively low levels of influence, they need to be closely tracked and steps should be taken to improve their knowledge about and perceptions of the company. The segmentation example also identified the importance of mothers who value choice for their families and noted the opportunity to turn their positive perceptions of the company into a valuable reputational asset by building a stronger relationship and reinforcing the company's strengths and values.[22]

Transparency

The McKinsey consultants admonished companies that while communications are essential to effective reputation management, at the end of the day, it is the actual deeds and actions of companies that have the great impact on stakeholder perceptions. A related notion is transparency, the regular practice of companies to fully share sufficient information, good and bad, about the environmental and social impacts of their operations with stakeholders. Stakeholders are demanding information about crucial business issues including the content and design of products, manufacturing processes, treatment of employees, and relationships with supply chain partners (and working conditions inside those partners), and they do not want the information to be served up solely as public

---

[22] Id. at 8.

relations hype. Transparency, in the form of sustainability reporting and other communications, can help convince stakeholders that the company is moving in the right direction or highlight gaps between stakeholder expectations and performance that need to be addressed by the company. Transparency can take many different forms including disclosure of data collected during trials for new products and public collaborations with competitors and other organizations to produce reports on issues that relate not only to the company but to the entire sector in which the company operates. Transparency should be mandatory during any period of reputational crisis; however, even when things are going well companies should communicate fully on their actions in order to build a reservoir of goodwill among stakeholders that can be tapped into at a later date when issues do arise.[23]

Engaging a Broad Group of Influencers

The McKinsey consultants acknowledged the ongoing importance of formal marketing and public relations activities in creating and defending corporate reputations; however, they urged companies to go beyond these tools and choose from the following list of methods for quickly and effectively spreading positive information and messages regarding the company's activities[24]"

- *War Room:* The purpose is to ensure an opportunity to refute critics and deliver messages in daily news cycles. Examples include media professionals' war room responsible for monitoring and responding to news. Desired outcomes include no attack left unanswered and responses to every reporter.
- *Free Media:* The purpose is to deliver messages through low-cost and highly trusted channels. Examples include speeches, events, press conferences, dissemination of research papers, company

---

[23] Id. at 9.
[24] Id. at 11.

blogging on specific issues, establishing communications with key stakeholders through participation in appropriate discussion boards, and creating and publicizing free interactive tools on the company website that customers can use for accessing information and solutions to problems such as energy conservation.

Desired outcomes include regularly creating new stories showing company in a favorable light and establishing relationships with opinion leaders.

- *Paid Media:* A supplement to free media, the purpose is to ensure that messages are delivered with maximum control of messaging and targeting. Examples include television, print ads, brochures, websites, and mailings. Desired outcomes include ensuring that everyone hears, sees, and reads the message.

- *Networking:* The purpose is to develop relationships with broad set of stakeholders and listen and deliver messages to them. Examples include meetings with opinion leaders, politicians, organizations (e.g., unions), media, and other stakeholders as well as two-way dialogues on a moderated discussion board established on the company's website. Desired outcomes include development and maintenance of a wide network of influential supporters and better understanding of detractors.

- *Giving:* The purpose is to reinforce messages through charitable contributions. Examples include the charitable focus of an outdoors fashion business on environmental causes. Desired outcome includes positive associations from working on good causes.

- *Operations:* The purpose is to reinforce messages and reduce reputational risks through activities within the business. Examples include Starbuck's free trade-certified coffee and supply chain policies and practices of various companies. Desired outcome includes seamless integration between company's actions and reputational consequences.

- *Partnerships:* The purpose is to gain credibility by working with others to solve industrywide reputation issues. An example is the effort to develop and implement labor certification standards in the textile industry. Desired outcome includes more friends to help in shared reputation battles.

- *Surrogates:* The purpose is to use high-credibility people to reinforce strategic messages. Examples include placing prominent people on the board of directors and in executive positions. Desired outcome includes star power speaking up for the company and its brand and reputation.
- *Grassroots:* The purpose is to leverage energy of current supporters. Examples include bumper stickers, blogs, and interactive websites that encourage visitors to work together with the company on a specific environmental or social issue (e.g., information on how consumer can conserve energy or improve their personal health and well-being). Desired outcome includes highly visible support for the company.

The fundamental assumption underlying many of the afore-listed methods is that credible third parties speaking positively about the company can be more effective than the company's internal marketing and public relations departments in improving the company's reputation and reinforcing the key strategic messages that the company wants to communicate to its stakeholders. The McKinsey consultants advised that companies cannot and should not rely on a single kind of approach for adequately addressing a threat to their reputation and that a mix of tactics should be developed and implemented by multidisciplinary and cross-functional teams in order to ensure that the response is properly coordinated throughout the company's strategy, operational activities, and communications methods. Reputation strategy and implementation should be led and coordinated by the CEO from the very topic of the organization, with assistance and oversight from a committee of the board of directors; however, the CEO needs to be supported by the leaders of other functions and departments throughout the company including regulatory affairs, legal, public relations and corporate communications, marketing, corporate social responsibility, investor relations, and information technology. Each of these specialists can bring to bear their specific knowledge of the needs and expectations of the stakeholders that fall under their purview. For example, the chief marketing officer should already have a good understanding of how customers view the company and what customers expect from the company in order to maintain their loyalty and advocate for the company's products and services to others. The information technology team should be able to provide assistance in developing and implementing the web-based communications strategies mentioned earlier in order to better engage with customers and other stakeholders and allow them to use interactive tools to access information about how the company contributes to solving important environmental and social issues.[25]

Reputation management is a rapidly evolving concept and has already become widely acknowledged as a valuable intangible asset that can become an important source of competitive advantage for companies, albeit an asset that can quickly be squandered or otherwise lost due to events that either could not be foreseen or which the company was inadequately prepared for. Reputation management also goes hand-in-hand with a company's branding activities, which are certainly important given that surveys repeatedly affirm that brand is an important component of corporate goodwill. A strong positive reputation also helps companies with recruiting and retaining talent. However, reputation management has been challenged on ethical grounds, particularly with respect to information and communications in the Internet, and companies need to be truthful and consistently transparent and own to their mistakes and demonstrate to stakeholders through their actions and words that they are committed to telling the whole story and sharing the journey toward resolving any reputational issues. Companies also need to resist the temptation to argue with critics during times of reputational crisis and remain focused on solving the problems that are immediately apparent to observers. Once mitigation and remediation is under control, the company can turn back to assessing why a problem may have arisen and share the results of that assessment with stakeholders in the form of a dialogue rather than a battle.

---

[25] Id. at 11–12.

Alternative Methods for Communicating Transparently

The benefits to the business of CSR and CSR reporting and communications differ from one company to the next, and must be assessed on a case-by-case basis. While most of the discussion in this publication has focused on frameworks for formalized sustainability reporting, companies can deploy transparency regarding their environmental and sociality responsibility in different ways both internally and externally depending on the size of their businesses, the sectors in which they operate and, most importantly, the unique requirements of their specific set of stakeholders. For example, according to a European Union publication[26]:

- Small and medium-sized enterprises (SMEs), which have few employees and are firmly rooted in the local community, often need to make no formal communication efforts in order to pass on information about their CSR. In that situation, employees, customers, and the local community know the entrepreneur personally and know about his or her company's commitment and behavior, and this makes it easier and more practical to pass information informally through direct contacts.
- In business-to-business (B2B) relationships and in the financial markets, transparency can be promoted by soliciting and answering targeted questions. Customer firms and socially responsible investment funds (and mainstream investors) routinely send their suppliers and portfolio companies questionnaires about their social responsibility and behavior; however, there is no generally recognized and standardized survey and assessment procedure in place. In addition, companies are increasingly asked about their corporate behavior by researchers, NGOs, consumer associations as well as individual citizens.

---

[26] *Handbook on Corporate Social Responsibility (CSR) for Employers' Organizations.* (European Union CSR for All Project, April 2014), 40–41.

- In business-to-customer (B2C) relationships, companies make considerable efforts through supplementary voluntary information on packaging, the label or in direct communication with consumers in order to provide them with information about the product and the production process. In addition, companies and consumers communicate regarding the company's CSR actions via websites, social media, contact forms, e-mails, or hotlines. CSR transparency is routinely utilized by companies to build their profile and image, and to appeal to customers who prioritize environmental and social responsibility when making their purchasing decisions.
- Companies organize workshops in order to come into contact with stakeholders to account for their activities and to discuss social as well as environmental issues.
- Via information to the press, companies report on new developments, initiatives, and projects.
- Via internal communication channels, companies regularly keep their employees informed.
- Companies present their experiences on CSR websites, in good practice compilations and through speaking engagements.

Even those companies that prepare a full-blown CSR or sustainability report will supplement that report with specialized reports on progress relating to specific commitments, such as the company's efforts to implement the principles of the UN Global Compact.

About the Author

The author of this book is **Alan S. Gutterman,** whose prolific output of practical guidance and tools for legal and financial professionals, managers, entrepreneurs, and investors has made him one of the best-selling individual authors in the global legal publishing marketplace. His cornerstone work, *Business Transactions Solution*, is an online-only product available and featured on Thomson Reuters' Westlaw, the world's largest legal content platform, which includes almost 200 book-length modules covering the entire lifecycle of a business. Alan has also authored or edited over 90 books on sustainable entrepreneurship, leadership and management, business law and transactions, international law and business, and technology management for a number of publishers including Thomson Reuters, Practical Law, Kluwer, Routledge, Aspatore, Oxford, Quorum, ABA Press, Aspen, Sweet & Maxwell, Euromoney, Harvard Business Publishing, CCH, and BNA. Alan is currently a partner of GCA Law Partners LLP in Mountain View CA (www.gcalaw.com) and has extensive experience as a partner and senior counsel with internationally recognized law firms counseling small and large business enterprises in the areas of general corporate and securities matters, venture capital, mergers and acquisitions, international law and transactions, strategic business alliances, technology transfers, and intellectual property, and has also held senior management positions with several technology-based businesses including service as the chief legal officer of a leading international distributor of IT products headquartered in Silicon Valley and as the chief operating officer of an emerging broadband media company. He has been an adjunct faculty member at several colleges and universities and has also launched the Sustainable Entrepreneurship Project (www.seproject. org) to teach and support individuals and companies, both startups and mature firms, seeking to create and build sustainable businesses based on purpose, innovation, shared value and respect for people and planet. He has also launched a projects relating to ageism.

Index

OTHER TITLES IN THE ENVIRONMENTAL AND SOCIAL SUSTAINABILITY FOR BUSINESS ADVANTAGE COLLECTION

Robert Sroufe, Duquesne University, Editor

- *Sustainability Leader in a Green Business Era* by Amr E. Sukkar
- *Managing Sustainability* by John Friedman
- *Human Resource Management for Organizational Sustainability* by Radha R. Sharma
- *Climate Change Management* by Huong Ha
- *Social Development Through Benevolent Business* by Kalyan Sankar Mandal
- *Developing Sustainable Supply Chains to Drive Value, Volume I* by Robert P. Sroufe and Steven A. Melnyk
- *Developing Sustainable Supply Chains to Drive Value, Volume II* by Robert P. Sroufe and Steven A. Melnyk
- *ISO 50001 Energy Management Systems* by Johannes Kals
- *Feasibility Analysis for Sustainable Technologies* by Scott R. Herriott
- *The Role of Legal Compliance in Sustainable Supply Chains, Operations, and Marketing* by John Wood
- *Change Management for Sustainability* by Huong Ha
- *The Thinking Executive's Guide to Sustainability* by Kerul Kassel
- *A Primer on Sustainability* by Ronald Whitfield and Jeanne McNett
- *IT Sustainability for Business Advantage* by Brian Moore
- *Developing Sustainable Supply Chains to Drive Value* by Robert Sroufe and Steven Melnyk

Concise and Applied Business Books

The Collection listed above is one of 30 business subject collections that Business Expert Press has grown to make BEP a premiere publisher of print and digital books. Our concise and applied books are for…

- Professionals and Practitioners
- Faculty who adopt our books for courses
- Librarians who know that BEP's Digital Libraries are a unique way to offer students ebooks to download not restricted with any digital rights management
- Executive Training Course Leaders
- Business Seminar Organizers

Business Expert Press books are for anyone who needs to dig deeper on business ideas, goals, and solutions to everyday problems. Whether one print book, one ebook, or buying a digital library of 110 ebooks, we remain the affordable and smart way to be business smart. For more information, please visit www.businessexpertpress.com, or contact sales@businessexpertpress.com.

www.ingramcontent.com/pod-product-compliance
Lightning Source LLC
Chambersburg PA
CBHW061322220326
41599CB00026B/4986